W9-BYB-188

The Confessions of Our Faith

The Westminster Confession of Faith
The Larger Catechism
The Shorter Catechism

The Fortress Edition

Historical Introduction
Dr. David B. Calhoun

Editor
Rev. Brian W. Kinney

Fortress Book Service & Publishers
www.fortressbookservice.com

Copyright 2007 by Fortress Book Service & Publishers

All rights reserved. No part of this book may be
reproduced in any form without written permission from:

Fortress Book Service & Publishers

800-241-4016

www.fortressbookservice.com

fortressbk@aol.com

Grateful acknowledgement is made to:

The Dean and Chapter of Westminster for permission to
use a picture of the Jerusalem Chamber and quotations;
Crossway/Goodnews Publishers for quotations from the
English Standard Version of the Bible; and Christy Rodriguez
for pictures of Westminster used in this publication.

ISBN-13: 978-0-9793718-0-6
ISBN-10: 0-9793718-0-5

Printed in the United States of America

Book design, layout, and production by Martha Nichols/aMuse Productions

TABLE OF CONTENTS

PREFACE

BY THE EDITOR,
THE REV. BRIAN KINNEY

"If you confess with your mouth that Jesus is Lord and believe in your heart that God raised him from the dead, you will be saved" (Romans 10:9). Thus the Apostle Paul tells us the importance of our confession of what Scripture testifies are the truths about Jesus Christ.

Yet how shall we know which truths are most important for us to confess? Surely we could confess all of the Bible, if we were capable even of remembering all the truths contained in the 66 books of God's revelation. Most of us, however, do much better with a summary of the central truths of the faith, a summary that we can hold in our hands and retain in its essence in our minds, perhaps even to memorize its doctrinal core. Such a summary is found in the great documents of the Reformation known as the Westminster Confession of Faith and the Larger and Shorter Catechisms.

What we present to you in this Fortress Edition are those three confessional writings, the doctrinal heart of the Reformed faith. These confessions are both for believers, who have them as a guide for life and faith, and for unbelievers, who need them in order to understand the teachings of Jesus Christ and to distinguish between the mandates of God and the opinions of man – and perhaps turn to God and be saved by confessing that Jesus is their Lord.

The Fortress Edition begins with the assumption that God's truths are eternal and universal. God is not a man that He should change His mind. However, the language of man does change over the centuries to the point at which some English words of the 1640s no longer are understood in the English speaking world, expressions such as "Therefore it pleased the Lord, at sundry times, and in divers manners. ..." Thus have we undertaken to follow standard English usage for clarity, while at the same time leaving the statement of doctrines unchanged. Specifically, we have avoided any changes to vital theological terms that bear heavily on our doctrinal standards, words such as predestination, election, justification, sanctification, propitiation, and the like, along with words such as recreations that have been at the center of doctrinal controversies. The councils and courts of our church are the forums for defining these terms, not the computer screen of an editor.

In our attempt to make the Westminster Confession and the Catechisms clearer to the 21st century reader, we hope that believers from various backgrounds will use them for an understanding of the central teachings of the Christian faith. Many Christians have so little understanding of systematic theology that they are almost helpless in the defense of what they believe. Yet the Confession and Catechisms are so thoroughly and solely based on Scripture that they provide a wonderful framework for the understanding and articulation of the message of the Bible. The writers of these documents have provided us with many "proof texts" from Scripture to support this framework. Therefore we have included the citations for the proof texts handed down to us from the Westminster Divines.

Editor's Note: Other than substituting standard English usage where necessary, our primary documents (the Burgess manuscript and the Caruthers edition of the Confessions) are the same as those approved by the First General Assembly of the Presbyterian Church in America in 1973. We are grateful to the PCA for their approval and official use of the Westminster Standards and to Crossway Bibles for permission to use quotations from the English Standard Version of the Bible.

Entrance to the Nave of Westminster Abbey, which has served as the coronation church of kings and queens for over a thousand years.

THE WESTMINSTER ASSEMBLY (1643–1648)

BY DR. DAVID B. CALHOUN

Professor of Church History and Chair of the Church
History and World Mission Department,
Covenant Theological Seminary, St. Louis, Missouri

Sixteenth-century Puritans were disappointed with the middle-of-the-road reform of the Church of England favored by Elizabeth I. Their successors had great hopes that the Scottish King James VI (who in 1603 became James I of England) would bring the Church of England into greater conformity with the Presbyterian Church in Scotland. Soon it became obvious that King James had no intention of doing this. In fact, he was determined to make Scotland's church more like the English church. Puritan disillusionment with James quickly became despair with Charles I, the son and successor of James, and with the fiercely anti-Puritan Archbishop William Laud.

Tensions heightened and fighting broke out in both Scotland and England. In 1638, the National Covenant rallied Presbyterian determination after the king's attempt to introduce a revised English *Book of Common Prayer* for Scottish worship. The Bishops' Wars of 1639 and 1640 failed to put down the uprising. In 1642, war erupted in England between the king and the Puritan Parliament (the so-called "Long Parliament" that began on November 3, 1640, and continued until dissolved by Oliver Cromwell on April 20, 1653). The Parliament insisted on a larger role in government against the royal absolutism of Charles, and greater reform in the church against Laud's high-church policies and Arminian doctrine. This Civil War was "not a selfish and ferocious conflict like the Wars of the Roses, but a war fought mainly for political and religious ideals."[1] It "made England at last the stronghold of

---

1   F. E. Halliday, *A Concise History of England*, 116.

constitutional liberty in Europe, and laid the foundation for a Protestant repub-
lic in America."[1] After some early uncertainty, the war resulted in victory for
the Parliament, and the executions of Archbishop Laud in 1645 and King
Charles I in 1649. Meanwhile, the hierarchy and liturgy of the Church of
England were abolished. "The old building was destroyed," comments Philip
Schaff, "before a new building was agreed upon."[2]

On May 13, 1643, the Parliament organized an assembly of ministers (or
"divines") to create standards for a Church of England that would be reformed
in worship, government, and doctrine. A few weeks later, on July 1, the
opening session of the Westminster Assembly was held, with both houses of
Parliament in attendance. The prolocutor (presiding officer), William Twisse,
preached from John 14:18—"I will not leave you comfortless: I will come to
you." The Assembly sent fraternal greetings to the Reformed churches in the
Netherlands, France, Switzerland, and elsewhere, and settled down to its
first task—a modest revision of the Thirty-Nine Articles to clarify or strengthen,
where necessary, the Reformed theology of these defining statements of
Anglican doctrine.

The Assembly comprised 151 members, including 30 laymen, chosen by
Parliament to represent the counties, the universities, the House of Lords, and
the House of Commons. Three of the divines were ministers of the Reformed
Church of France, serving congregations in Canterbury and London. Three
New England ministers were invited to take part, but declined to make the
long journey. Twenty-eight of the divines did not attend (mainly because of
the king's prohibition), and twenty-one, called "superadded divines," were
appointed later to replace members who did not attend or who died during
the proceedings. Some outstanding Puritan pastors and theologians, such as
Richard Baxter and John Owen, were not included in the Assembly list. A

---

1   Philip Schaff, The Creeds of Christendom 1: 702-703.
2   Schaff 1:734.

few months later, eight commissioners were chosen by the Church of Scotland "to propone [put forward], consult, treat and conclude" with the Westminster divines. The Scots arrived in London "fresh from the battle 'with lordly bishops, popish ceremonies, and royal mandates.'"[1]

The Westminster divines, mostly teachers and pastors of churches, were described by the Parliament as "learned, godly, and judicious." And they were. "Puritanism had been doing its work of making great men in England for a century."[2] Richard Baxter held that "the Christian world, since the days of the Apostles, had never a synod of more excellent divines" than Westminster and the Synod of Dort.[3] Church historian Philip Schaff wrote that "not a few" of the Westminster divines "combined rare learning, eloquence, and piety in beautiful harmony."[4] John Leith described the Westminster divines as "very competent men, as competent as composed any synod in Church history."[5] William Barker's *Puritan Profiles* summarizes the lives and accomplishments of many of the Westminster divines (and some other influential Puritans who lived during the time of the Westminster Assembly).

The Assembly's members were all Calvinists in theology and could all be called Puritans in the broad sense. The main difference among them was in their views of church government and discipline. This resulted in a number of groups or parties—moderate Episcopalians (most of whom declined to attend out of loyalty to the king), Presbyterians (much the largest group), and Congregationalists (who gained influence through the growing support of Oliver Cromwell and the army). There was a small but learned group of Erastians who held that church discipline was to be carried out only with approval of the state.

1 Schaff 1:745.
2 "The Origin and Formation of the Westminster Confession of Faith," prepared for the 1906 General Assembly of the Presbyterian Church in the United States of America. Reprinted in The Westminster Confession of Faith (Atlanta: Committee for Christian Education & Publications, 1990), xv.
3 William Barker, Puritan Profiles, 288. Schaff 1:729.
4 Schaff 1:740.
5 John Leith, Assembly at Westminster: Reformed Theology in the Making, 49.

The Assembly met at first in Westminster Abbey's imposing Henry VII Chapel, its ornate medieval architecture and decoration forming a striking contrast to Puritan simplicity of worship and dress. As the weather turned cooler, the divines were glad to move to the more comfortable Jerusalem Chamber. Every member took a vow (which was read every Monday morning) to "maintain nothing in point of doctrine but what I believe to be most agreeable to the Word of God; nor in point of discipline, but what may make most for God's glory and the peace and good of his Church." The Assembly met every day except Saturday and Sunday, from nine o'clock until one or two. Forty members constituted a quorum. In the afternoons, the divines worked in committees. One of the rules guiding the deliberations required that "what any man undertakes to prove as necessary, he shall make good out of Scripture." The minutes and other reports of the Assembly's work reveal a strong commitment to this rule.

Much of the time of the Westminster divines was taken up with preaching and hearing sermons. More than 240 sermons were delivered to the Parliament during the 1640s, most of them by members of the Westminster Assembly. Because of their efforts to apply Scripture to their times, these preachers have been called "England's Deuteronomists." Many hours were spent in corporate prayer and discussion concerning the lessons of God's providence in the successes and failures of the Parliamentary army and the progress or lack thereof of the Assembly itself. Scottish commissioner Robert Baillie described the "fast" observed on May 17, 1644, as "the sweetest day" he had spent in England, although the prayers, psalms, and sermons of that day lasted eight hours without interruption. "We cannot read such accounts," Schaff comments, "without amazement at the devotional fervor and endurance of the Puritan divines."[1]

1   Schaff 1:752.

There were 1,163 numbered sessions of the Westminster Assembly, the last coming on February 22, 1649 (although the doctrinal standards were completed by 1648). For several more years the Assembly continued as a ministerial examining committee. It was never formally dissolved.

The Westminster Assembly's first project of revising the Thirty-Nine Articles was abandoned, and work on new documents begun, after the Presbyterians of Scotland joined with the English Puritans in August 1643 in the *Solemn League and Covenant* for "the preservation of the reformed religion in the Church of Scotland ... the reformation of religion in the kingdoms of England and Ireland, in doctrine, worship, discipline, and government, according to the Word of God, and the example of the best reformed churches."

Over the course of five and a half years, during a time of political and religious chaos, the Westminster Assembly created five great documents of theological orthodoxy and ecclesiastical stability for the church in England, Ireland, and Scotland.

The Directory for Public Worship set forth a middle ground between a fixed liturgy and a completely open form of worship in which everyone would be "left to his own will." The *Directory* contains what has been called "the finest brief description of expository preaching to be found in the English language."[1] The divines also approved Francis Rous's revised version of the Psalter for congregational worship.

The Form of Church Government set forth a Presbyterian polity tempered by the debate between the Presbyterians and the competent and outspoken small group of Independents (their leaders were called "the five dissenting brethren" by the Presbyterians). It was tempered as well by the disagreement between the stricter Presbyterians who insisted on the "divine right" of Presbyterianism, and others who held that Presbyterian polity was "lawful and agreeable to the Word of God," but subject to change according to the needs of the church.

---

1   S. B. Ferguson, *Dictionary of Scottish Church History and Theology*, 864.

The Westminster Confession of Faith, the Assembly's most important work, is a model of mainstream Calvinism, setting forth what B. B. Warfield called "the generic doctrine of the Reformed churches."[1] Drawing on the richness of the creeds and confessions of church history, especially the Thirty-Nine Articles, the Lambeth Articles, and the Irish Articles of Archbishop James Ussher (one of the greatest "doctrinal Puritans" of the time, who though not in attendance at Westminster was present "in spirit"), the Westminster divines with "remarkable comprehensiveness, balance and precision"[2] summed up in thirty-three chapters "what man is to believe concerning God, and what duty God requires of man."[3] The *Confession* is noted for its strong opening chapter on the authority of the Scripture, its uncompromising allegiance to God's sovereignty in providence and predestination, its covenant theology, its Protestant and evangelical soteriology, its unique chapter on adoption, and its emphasis on the Christian life—both personal and communal. Chapters 10 through 33, comprising two-thirds of the Confession, deal with the Christian life (supplemented by the substantial commentary on the Ten Commandments in the *Larger Catechism*.) It is abundantly clear that the creators of the Westminster standards "were not simply concerned with sound doctrine but also with the embodiment of doctrine in life."[4]

The *Confession* was presented to Parliament for approval in December 1646. Fifteen hundred "proof texts" were added (by order of Parliament), and the complete document was published, with the title *The Humble Advice of the Assembly of Divines, Now by Authority of Parliament sitting at Westminster, concerning a Confession of Faith*. After further discussion, Parliament published another "authorized" edition of the *Confession*, with the new title of "Articles of Religion approved and passed by both Houses of Parliament." It differed from the Assembly's *Confession* by the omission of

---

1   B. B. Warfield, *The Westminster Assembly and Its Work*, 96.
2   David F. Wright, *New Dictionary of Theology*, 156.
3   *Westminster Shorter Catechism*, question 3.
4   John Leith, *Assembly at Westminster*, 97.

parts of chapters 20 and 24 and all of chapters 30 and 31, touching on issues of church–state relations and responsibilities.

The Westminster Assembly produced two catechisms—"one more exact and comprehensive, another more easy and short for new beginners." *The Larger Catechism* was completed in October 1647, and *The Shorter Catechism* a month later. *The Shorter Catechism*, originally intended for children and beginners, made the greater impact and remains a beloved expression of Reformed doctrine. For millions of children (and adults) it laid what John G. Paton (nineteenth-century missionary to the New Hebrides from Scotland's Reformed Presbyterian Church) called "the solid rock-foundations" of their Christian lives.[1] The famous *New England Primer*, for more than a hundred years the beginning textbook for America's children, contained *The Shorter Catechism*. An 1843 printing of the *Primer* states:

> Our Puritan fathers brought the Shorter Catechism with them across the ocean and laid it on the same shelf with the family Bible. They taught it diligently to their children. … If in this catechism the true and fundamental doctrines of the Gospel are expressed in fewer and better words and definitions than in any other summary, why ought we not now to train up a child in the way he should go?[2]

The Westminster Confession served, in a limited way, the church in England until the Restoration in 1660 (although Presbyterianism functioned effectively, it seems, only in London and Lancashire). The General Assembly of the Church of Scotland received the *Confession* as its theological standard (alongside the Scots Confession of 1560) on August 27, 1647. The General Assembly declared it "to be most agreeable to the Word of God, and in nothing contrary to the received doctrine, worship, discipline, and government of this Kirk," and thankfully acknowledged the great mercy of the Lord "in that so excellent a Confession of Faith is prepared, and thus far agreed

1   James Paton, ed., *John G. Paton—Missionary to the New Hebrides: An Autobiography (1889, 1965)*, 16.
2   *The New-England Primer* (1777, 1991), 4.

upon in both kingdoms." *The Westminster Confession,* with modifications in church polity, was adopted in 1648 by the Congregational churches of Massachusetts, as their *Cambridge Platform.* It was adopted as the *Savoy Declaration* by the English Congregational churches in 1658. *The Westminster Confession,* altered in baptism as well as polity, was accepted by the London Baptists in 1677 and, as *The Philadelphia Confession,* by Baptists in America in 1742. In 1729 the newly organized Presbyterian Church in the American colonies adopted *The Westminster Confession* ("good forms of sound words," they called it), with the provision that ministers could take exceptions to the *Confession,* provided the presbytery agreed that those exceptions did not compromise the theological integrity of the *Confession.* *The Westminster Confession* was amended in chapters 20, 23, and 31 (dealing with issues of church and state) by the American Presbyterian Church and approved in 1789 at its first General Assembly.

The Westminster Confession has been translated into many languages (most recently into Lithuanian) and has shaped Reformed churches and thought throughout the world. Its "solidity and majesty"[1] have inspired many people, and its biblical faithfulness has helped them to know "how we may glorify and enjoy" God.

In 1843, Princeton Seminary's Archibald Alexander wrote concerning *The Westminster Confession and Catechisms:*

> We venerate these standards, partly because they embody the wisdom of an august Synod; because they come down to us associated with the memory and faith of saints and martyrs and embalmed with their blood; but we love them most of all because they contain the truth of God—that truth which forms the foundation of our hopes. As our fathers prized them, and we prize them, so may our children and our children's children love and preserve them.[2]

1   David F. Wright, *New Dictionary of Theology,* 156.
2   *Biblical Repertory and Princeton Review* (1843), 586.

In his opening address to Princeton Seminary students on September 20, 1903, B. B. Warfield recommended some books that the students should read in order to nurture their spiritual life. He ended, somewhat surprisingly, with the statement that the *Creeds of Christendom* are "more directly, richly, and evangelically devotional" than any other writings, apart from the Bible. He recommended especially *The Westminster Confession of Faith* and *The Heidelberg Catechism*. Warfield said: "He who wishes to grow strong in his religious life, let him, I say, next to the Bible, feed himself on the great creeds of the church." They are not "metaphysical speculation," said Warfield, but "compressed and weighted utterances of the Christian heart."[1]

John Murray paid high tribute to *The Westminster Confession of Faith* when he wrote that "in respect to fidelity to Scripture, precision of thought and formulation, fullness of statement, balanced proportion of emphasis, studied economy of words, and effective exposure of error, no creedal confession attains to the same level of excellence characterizing that of Westminster." Murray revealed his Protestant and Presbyterian convictions when he added that this praise did not mean that the confession was "a perfect document" and "not susceptible to improvement or correction ... an estimate and veneration that belong only to the Word of God."[2]

---

1   *Shorter Works of Benjamin B. Warfield* 2:492-94.
2   *Collected Writings of John Murray* 4:241-63.

Prayer

*Our Father, we thank you that you have given us your own
counsel in the inspired Scripture concerning those things which
we need to know for your glory and our salvation—and that by your
singular care and providence you have kept that Scripture pure in all ages.*

*We thank you for the inward illumination of the Holy Spirit that enables us to
come to the saving knowledge of those things that are revealed in your Word.*

*We thank you that for the better government and further
edification of the church you raised up assemblies
such as the one that met at Westminster Abbey.*

*Help us, our Father, to profit from its diligent example and learn
from its careful documents, while always remembering that the
Supreme Judge by which all controversies of religion are to be determined,
all theologies are to be examined, and in whose sentence we are to rest,
is no other than the Holy Spirit speaking in the Scripture.*

*In Jesus's name we pray, in obedience to His commands,
and with confidence in His promises.*

Amen.

BRIEF BIBLIOGRAPHY

Barker, William S. *Puritan Profiles: 54 Influential Puritans at the Time When the Westminster Confession of Faith was Written* (1996).

Carson, John L., and Hall, David W., eds. *To Glorify and Enjoy God: A Commemoration of the 350th Anniversary of the Westminster Assembly* (1994).

Leith, John H. *Assembly at Westminster: Reformed Theology in the Making* (1973).

Warfield, Benjamin Breckinridge. *The Westminster Assembly and Its Work* (1931).

The Westminster Confession of Faith

The Jerusalem Chamber was ... the meeting place of the Westminster Assembly, the committee of divines appointed by Parliament in 1643 to reform the Church of England. Among the documents to emerge from the Assembly was the Westminster Confession, which was to be the definitive doctrinal statement of English Presbyterianism.

—The Dean and Chapter of Westminster

CHAPTER 1

OF THE HOLY SCRIPTURE.

1. Although the light of nature, and the works of creation and providence do so far make known the goodness, wisdom, and power of God, as to leave men without excuse,[1] they are not sufficient to give that knowledge of God, and of his will, that is necessary for salvation.[2] Therefore it pleased the Lord, at various times, and in a variety of ways, to reveal Himself, and to declare His will to His Church;[3] and afterward, for the better preserving and propagating of the truth, and for the more sure establishment and comfort of the Church against the corruption of the flesh, and the malice of Satan and of the world,[4] to commit His same will to writing: which makes the Holy Scripture to be most necessary;[5] those former ways of God's revealing His will to His people being now ceased.[6]

2. Under the name of Holy Scripture, or the Word of God written, are now contained all the books of the Old and New Testaments, which are these,

---

1   Romans 1:19-20; 1:32; 2:1; 2:14-15; Psalm 19:1-3.
2   1 Corinthians 1:21; 2:13-14.
3   Hebrews 1:1.
4   Proverbs 22:19-21; Isaiah 8:19-20; Matthew 4:4,7,10; Luke 1:3-4; Romans 15:4.
5   2 Timothy 3:15; 2 Peter 1:19.
6   Hebrews 1:1-2.

2

OF THE OLD TESTAMENT

Genesis	Ecclesiastes
Exodus	The Song of Songs
Leviticus	Isaiah
Numbers	Jeremiah
Deuteronomy	Lamentations
Joshua	Ezekiel
Judges	Daniel
Ruth	Hosea
1 Samuel	Joel
2 Samuel	Amos
1 Kings	Obadiah
2 Kings	Jonah
1 Chronicles	Micah
2 Chronicles	Nahum
Ezra	Habakkuk
Nehemiah	Zephaniah
Esther	Haggai
Job	Zechariah
Psalms	Malachi
Proverbs	

OF THE NEW TESTAMENT

Matthew	1 Timothy
Mark	2 Timothy
Luke	Titus
John	Philemon
Acts	Hebrews
Romans	James
1 Corinthians	1 Peter
2 Corinthians	2 Peter
Galatians	1 John
Ephesians	2 John
Philippians	3 John
Colossians	Jude
1 Thessalonians	Revelation
2 Thessalonians	

All which are given by inspiration of God to be the rule of faith and life.[1]

---

1   Luke 16:29,31; 2 Timothy 3:16; Ephesians 2:20; Revelation 22:18-19

3. The books commonly called Apocrypha, not being of divine inspiration, are no part of the canon of the Scripture, and therefore are of no authority in the Church of God, nor to be any otherwise approved, or made use of, than other human writings.[1]

4. The authority of the Holy Scripture, for which it ought to be believed, and obeyed, depends not on the testimony of any man, or Church; but wholly on God (who is truth itself) the author thereof: and therefore it is to be received, because it is the Word of God.[2]

5. We may be moved and induced by the testimony of the Church to a high and reverend esteem of the Holy Scripture.[3] And the heavenliness of the matter, the efficacy of the doctrine, the majesty of the style, the unity of all the parts, the purpose of the whole (which is, to give all glory to God), the full revelation it makes of the only way of man's salvation, the many other incomparable excellencies, and the entire perfection thereof, are abundant evidence that Holy Scripture is the Word of God: yet our full persuasion and assurance of its infallible truth and divine authority is from the inward work of the Holy Spirit bearing witness by and with the Word in our hearts.[4]

6. The whole counsel of God concerning all things necessary for His own glory, man's salvation, faith and life, is either expressly set down in Scripture, or by good and necessary logic may be shown from Scripture: to which nothing at any time is to be added, whether by new revelations of the Spirit or traditions of men.[5] Nevertheless, we acknowledge the inward illumination of the Spirit of God to be necessary for the saving understanding of such things as are revealed in the Word:[6] and that there are some circumstances concerning the worship of God, and government of the Church, that arise from time to time and which are to be decided according to natural principles governed by a Christian heart, according to the general rules of the Word, which are always to be observed.[7]

1 Luke 22:27,44; Romans 3:2; 2 Peter 1:21.
2 1 Thessalonians 2:13; 2 Timothy 3:16; 2 Peter 1:19,21; 1 John 5:9.
3 1 Timothy 3:15.
4 Isaiah 54:21; John 16:13-14; 1 Corinthians 2:10-12; 1 John 2:20.
5 Galatians 1:8-9; 2 Thessalonians 2:2; 2 Timothy 3:15-17;
6 John 6:45; 1 Corinthians 2:9-12.
7 1 Corinthians 11:13-14; 14:26,40.

4

7. All things in Scripture are not equally obvious, nor equally clear to everyone:[1] yet those things that are necessary to be known, believed, and observed for salvation, are so clearly stated and explained in some place of Scripture or other, that not only the learned, but the unlearned, by paying reasonable attention, may attain a sufficient understanding of them.[2]

8. The Old Testament in Hebrew (which was the native language of the people of God of old), and the New Testament in Greek (which, at the time of the writing of it, was most generally known to the nations), being immediately inspired by God, and, by His special care and providence, kept pure in all ages, are therefore authentic;[3] so as, in all controversies of religion, the Church is to appeal ultimately to them.[4] But, because these original languages are not known to all the people of God, who have the right to read and the desire to know the Scriptures, and are commanded, in the fear of God, to read and search them,[5] therefore they are to be translated into the common language of every nation where they are brought,[6] that, the Word of God dwelling plentifully in all, they may worship Him in an acceptable manner;[7] and, through patience and comfort of the Scriptures, may have hope.[8]

9. The infallible rule of interpretation of Scripture is the Scripture itself: and therefore, when there is a question about the true and full sense of any Scripture (which is not multiple, but one), it must be searched and known by other places that speak more clearly.[9]

10. The supreme judge by which all controversies of religion are to be determined, and all decrees of councils, opinions of ancient writers, doctrines of men, and private illuminations are to be examined, and on whose decisions we are to rely, can be no other but the Holy Spirit speaking in the Scripture.[10]

---

1   2 Peter 3:16.
2   Psalm 119:105,130.
3   Matthew 5:18.
4   Isaiah 8:20; John 5:39,46; Acts 25:15.
5   John 5:39.
6   1 Corinthians 14:6,9,11-12,24,27-28.
7   Colossians 3:16.
8   Romans 15:4.
9   Acts 15:15-16; 2 Peter 1:20-21.
10 Matthew 22:29,31; Acts 28:25; Ephesians 2:20.

CHAPTER 11

OF GOD, AND OF THE HOLY TRINITY.

1. There is but one only,[1] living, and true God,[2] who is infinite in being and perfection,[3] a most pure spirit,[4] invisible,[5] without body, parts,[6] or human frailty;[7] unchangeable,[8] immense,[9] eternal,[10] incomprehensible,[11] almighty,[12] most wise,[13] most holy,[14] most free,[15] most absolute;[16] working all things according to the counsel of His own unchangeable and most righteous will,[17] for His own glory;[18] most loving,[19] gracious, merciful, patient, abundant in goodness and truth, forgiving iniquity, transgression, and sin;[20] the one who rewards those who diligently seek Him;[21] and along with this, most just, and terrifying in His judgments,[22] hating all sin,[23] and who will by no means acquit the guilty.[24]

2. God has all life,[25] glory,[26] goodness,[27] blessedness,[28] in and of Himself; and is alone in and of Himself all-sufficient, not standing in need of any creatures which He has made,[29] nor deriving any glory from them,[30] but only displaying His own glory in, by, to, and upon them. He is the only fountain of all being, of whom, through whom, and to whom are all things[31] and has most sovereign dominion over them, to do by them, for them, or upon them whatever pleases Him.[32] In His sight all things are

1 Deuteronomy 6:4; 1 Corinthians 8:4-6.
2 Jeremiah 10:10; 1 Thessalonians 1:9.
3 Job 11:7-9; 26:14.
4 John 4:24.
5 1 Timothy 1:17.
6 Deuteronomy 4:15-16; Luke 24:39; John 4:24.
7 Acts 14:11,15.
8 Malachi 3:6; James 1:17.
9 1 Kings 8:27; Jeremiah 23:23-24.
10 Psalm 40:2; 1 Timothy 1:17.
11 Psalm 145:3.
12 Genesis 17:1; Revelation 4:8.
13 Romans 16:27.
14 Isaiah 6:3; Revelation 4:8.
15 Psalm 115:3.
16 Exodus 3:14.
17 Ephesians 1:11.
18 Proverbs 16:4; Romans 11:36.
19 1 John 4:8-16.
20 Exodus 34:6-7.
21 Hebrews 11:6.
22 Nahum 9:32-33
23 Psalm 5:5-6
24 Exodus 34:7; Nahum 1:2-3.
25 John 5:26.
26 Acts 7:2.
27 Psalm 119:68.
28 Romans 9:5; 1 Timothy 6:15.
29 Acts 17:24-25.
30 Job 22:2-3
31 Romans 11:36.
32 Daniel 4:25,35; 1 Timothy 6:15; Revelation 4:11.

open and known,[1] His knowledge is infinite, infallible, and independent of the creature,[2] so as nothing is to Him contingent, or uncertain.[3] He is most holy in all His counsels, in all His works, and in all His commands.[4] To Him is due from angels and men, and every other creature, whatever worship, service, or obedience He is pleased to require of them.[5]

3. In the unity of the Godhead there are three persons, of one substance, power, and eternity: God the Father, God the Son, and God the Holy Spirit:[6] the Father is not created by another, nor is He begotten or proceeding; the Son is eternally begotten of the Father;[7] the Holy Ghost is eternally proceeding from the Father and the Son.[8]

---

1   Hebrews 4:13.
2   Psalm 147:5; Romans 11:33-34.
3   Ezekiel 11:5; Acts 15:18.
4   Psalm 145:17; Romans 7:12.
5   Revelation 5:12-14.
6   Matthew 3:16-17; 28:19; 2 Corinthians 13:14; 1 John 5:7.
7   John 1:14,18.
8   John 15:26; Galatians 4:6.

CHAPTER III

OF GOD'S ETERNAL DECREE.

1. God from all eternity did, by the most wise and holy counsel of His own will, freely and unchangeably ordain whatever comes to pass.[1] Yet neither is God the author of sin;[2] nor are creatures forced to act contrary to their wills; nor is the liberty or contingency of second causes taken away, but rather established.[3]

2. Although God knows whatever may or can come to pass under all hypothetical conditions,[4] He has not decreed anything because He foresaw it as future, or as that which would come to pass under such conditions.[5]

3. By the decree of God, for the display of His glory, some men and angels[6] are predestined to everlasting life; and others foreordained to everlasting death.[7]

4. These angels and men, thus predestined and foreordained, are individually and unchangeably designed, and their number so certain and definite, that it cannot be either increased or decreased.[8]

5. Those of mankind who are predestined to life, God, before the foundation of the world was laid, according to His eternal and unchangeable purpose and the secret counsel and good pleasure of His will, chose in Christ for everlasting glory,[9] out of His mere free grace and love, without foreseeing faith, or good works, or perseverance in either faith or works, or any other quality of the creature, as conditions or causes moving Him to do so;[10] and all to the praise of His glorious grace.[11]

1   Romans 9:15,18; 11:33; Ephesians 1:11; Hebrews 6:17.
2   James 1:13,17; 1 John 1:5.
3   Proverbs 16:33; Matthew 17:12; John 19:11; Acts 2:23; 4:27-28.
4   1Samuel 23:11-12; Matthew 11:21,23; Acts 15:18.
5   Romans 9:11,13,16,18.
6   Matthew 25:41; 1 Timothy 5:21.
7   Proverbs 16:4; Romans 9:22-23; Ephesians 1:5-6.
8   John 13:18; 2 Timothy 2:19.
9   Romans 8:30; Ephesians 1:4,9,11; 1 Thessalonians 5:9; 2 Timothy 1:9.
10 Romans 9:11,13,16; Ephesians 1:4,9.
11 Ephesians 1:6,12.

6. As God has appointed the elect to glory, so has He, by the eternal and most free purpose of His will, foreordained all the means to accomplish this.[1] They who are elected, being fallen in Adam, are redeemed by Christ;[2] are effectually called to faith in Christ by His Spirit working in due time; and are justified, adopted, sanctified,[3] and kept by His power, through faith, for salvation.[4] None are redeemed by Christ, effectually called, justified, adopted, sanctified, and saved, but the elect only.[5]

7. The rest of mankind God was willing, according to the unsearchable counsel of His own will, by which He extends or witholds mercy as He pleases, for the glory of His sovereign power over His creatures, to pass by and to ordain to dishonor and wrath for their sin, to the praise of His glorious justice.[6]

8. The doctrine of this high mystery of predestination is to be handled with special prudence and care,[7] so that men, seeking to know the will of God revealed in His Word, and yielding obedience to it, may, from the certainty of their effectual calling, be assured of their eternal election.[8] So shall this doctrine bring praise, reverence, and admiration of God;[9] and humility, diligence, and abundant consolation to all who sincerely obey the Gospel.[10]

1 Ephesians 1:4-5; 2:10; 2 Thessalonians 2:13; 1 Peter 1:2.
2 1 Thessalonians 5:9-10; Titus 2:14.
3 Romans 8:30; Ephesians 1:5; 2 Thessalonians 2:13.
4 1 Peter 1:5.
5 John 6:64-65; 8:47; 10:26; 17:9; Romans 8:28; 1 John 2:19.

6 Matthew 11:25-26; Romans 9:17-18,21-22; 2 Timothy 2:19-20; 1 Peter 2:8; Jude 4.
7 Deuteronomy 29:29; Romans 9:20; 11:33.
8 2 Peter 1:10.
9 Romans 11:33; Ephesians 1:6.
10 Luke 10:20; Romans 8:33; 11:5,6,20; 2 Peter 1:10.

CHAPTER IV

OF CREATION.

1. It pleased God the Father, Son, and Holy Ghost,[1] for the display of the glory of His eternal power, wisdom, and goodness,[2] in the beginning, to create, or make out of nothing, the world, and all things in it whether visible or invisible, in the space of six days; and all very good.[3]

2. After God had made all other creatures, He created man, male and female,[4] with reasoning minds and immortal souls,[5] having knowledge, righteousness, and true holiness, after His own image,[6] having the law of God written in their hearts,[7] and power to fulfill it:[8] and yet with the possibility of transgressing, being left to the liberty of their own will, which was subject to change.[9] Besides this law written in their hearts, they received a command, not to eat of the Tree of the Knowledge of Good and Evil,[10] which while they kept, they were happy in their communion with God and had authority over the creatures.[11]

---

1 Genesis 1:2; Job 26:13; 33:4; John 1:2-3; Hebrews 1:2.
2 Psalm 33:5-6; 104:24; Jeremiah 10:12; Romans 1:20.
3 Genesis 1; Acts 17:24; Colossians 1:16; Hebrews 11:3.
4 Genesis 1:27.
5 Genesis 2:7; Ecclesiastes 12:7; Matthew 10:28; Luke 23:43.
6 Genesis 1:26; Ephesians 4:24; Colossians 3:10.
7 Romans 2:14-15.
8 Ecclesiastes 7:29.
9 Genesis 3:6; Ecclesiastes 7:29.
10 Genesis 2:17; 3:8-11,23.
11 Genesis 1:26,28.

CHAPTER V

OF PROVIDENCE.

1. God the great Creator of all things does uphold,[1] direct, make willing, and govern all creatures, actions, and things,[2] from the greatest even to the least,[3] by His most wise and holy providence,[4] according to His infallible foreknowledge,[5] and the free and unchangeable counsel of His own will,[6] to the praise of the glory of His wisdom, power, justice, goodness, and mercy.[7]

2. Although, in relation to the foreknowledge and decree of God, the first Cause, all things happen as God intended, without change and without fail;[8] yet, by the same providence, He orders them to come about through second causes, either necessarily, freely, or contingently.[9]

3. God, in His ordinary providence, makes use of means,[10] yet is free to work without,[11] above,[12] and against them,[13] at His pleasure.

4. The almighty power, unsearchable wisdom, and infinite goodness of God make themselves known in His providence, such that it extends itself even to the first fall, and all other sins of angels and men;[14] and that not merely by God's permission,[15] but such as has joined with it a most wise and powerful setting of limits,[16] and otherwise establishing of order, and governing of them, in many ways, to His own holy ends;[17] yet so, as this sinfulness proceeds only from the creature, and not from God, who, being most holy and righteous, neither is nor can be the author or approver of sin.[18]

---

1   Hebrews 1:3.
2   Job 38; 39; 40; 41; Psalm 135:6; Daniel 4:34-35; Acts 17:25-26,28.
3   Matthew 10:29-31.
4   Psalm 104:24; 145:17; Proverbs 15:3.
5   Psalm 94:8-11; Acts 15:18.
6   Ephesians 1:11.
7   Genesis 45:7; Psalm 145:7; Isaiah 63:14; Romans 9:17; Ephesians 3:10.
8   Acts 2:23.
9   Genesis 8:22; Exodus 21:13; Deuteronomy 19:5; 1 Kings 22:28,34; Isaiah 10:6-7; Jeremiah 31:35.
10 Isaiah 55:10-11; Acts 27:31,44.
11 Job 34:10; Hosea 1:7; Matthew 4:4.
12 Romans 9:19-21.
13 2 Kings 6:6; Daniel 3:27.
14 2 Samuel 16:10; 24:1; 1 Kings 22:22-23; 1 Chronicles 10:4,13-14; 21:1; Acts 2:23; Romans 11:32-34.
15 Acts 14:16.
16 2 Kings 19:28; Psalm 76:10.
17 Genesis 50:20; Isaiah 10:6-7,12.
18 Psalm 50:21; James 1:13-14,17; 1 John 2:16.

5. The most wise, righteous, and gracious God does often leave, for a time, His own children to many temptations, and the corruption of their own hearts, to chastise them for their former sins, or to show them the hidden strength of corruption and deceitfulness of their hearts, that they may be humbled;[1] and, to raise them to a more close and constant dependence for their support on Him, and to make them more watchful against all future occasions of sin, and for various other just and holy ends.[2]

6. As for those wicked and ungodly men whom God, as a righteous Judge, for former sins, does blind and harden,[3] from them He not only withholds His grace through which they might have been enlightened in their understandings, and convicted in their hearts;[4] but sometimes also withdraws the gifts that they had,[5] and exposes them to such objects as their corruption make occasions for sin;[6] and, with this, gives them over to their own lusts, the temptations of the world, and the power of Satan,[7] so that they harden themselves, even under those means that God uses for the softening of others.[8]

7. As the providence of God does, in general, reach to all creatures; so, after a most special manner, it takes care of His Church, and works all things to the good of it.[9]

---

1 2 Samuel 24:1; 2 Chronicles 32:25-26,31.
2 Psalm 73: 77:1,10,12; Mark 14:66-72;
   John 21:15-17; 2 Corinthians 12:7-9.
3 Romans 1:24,26,28; 11:7-8.
4 Deuteronomy 29:4.
5 Matthew 13:12; 25:29.
6 Deuteronomy 2:30; 2 Kings 8:12-13.

7 Psalm 81:11-12; 2 Thessalonians 2:10-12.
8 Exodus 7:3; 8:15,31; Isaiah 6:9-10; 8:14;
   Acts 28:26-27; 2 Corinthians 2:15-16;
   1 Peter 2:7-8.
9 Isaiah 43:3-5,14; Amos 9:8-9; Romans 8:28;
   1 Timothy 4:10.

CHAPTER VI

OF THE FALL OF MAN, OF SIN, AND OF THE PUNISHMENT THEREOF.

1. Our first parents, being seduced by the cunning and temptation of Satan, sinned, in eating the forbidden fruit.[1] This sin, God was willing, according to His wise and holy counsel, to permit, having intended it for His own glory.[2]

2. By this sin they fell from their original righteousness and communion, with God,[3] and so became dead in sin,[4] and wholly defiled in all the parts and faculties of soul and body.[5]

3. They being the root of all mankind, the guilt of this sin was imputed;[6] and the same death in sin, and corrupted nature, conveyed to all their descendants by ordinary generation.[7]

4. From this original corruption, whereby we are utterly indisposed, disabled, and opposite to all good,[8] and wholly inclined to all evil,[9] do proceed all actual transgressions.[10]

5. This corruption of nature, during this life, does remain in those who are regenerated;[11] and although it be, through Christ, pardoned, and subdued; yet both it, and all the passions it arouses, are truly sin.[12]

6. Every sin, both original and actual, being a transgression of the righteous law of God, and contrary to it,[13] does in its own nature bring guilt on the sinner,[14] so that he is bound over to the wrath of God,[15] and curse of the law,[16] and so made subject to death,[17] with all miseries spiritual,[18] temporal,[19] and eternal.[20]

---

1   Genesis 3:13; 2 Corinthians 11:3.
2   Romans 11:32.
3   Genesis 3:6-8; Ecclesiastes 7:29; Romans 3:23.
4   Genesis 2:17; Ephesians 2:1.
5   Genesis 6:5; Jeremiah 17:9; Romans 3:10-18; Titus 1:15.
6   Genesis 1:27-28; 2:16-17; Acts 17:26; Romans 5:12,15-19; 1 Corinthians 15:21-22,45,49.
7   Genesis 5:3; Job 14:4; 15:14; Psalm 51:5.
8   Romans 5:6; 7:18; 8:7; Colossians 1:21.
9   Genesis 6:5; 8:21; Romans 3:10-12.
10 Matthew 15:19; Ephesians 2:2-3; James 1:14-15.
11 Proverbs 20:9; Ecclesiastes 7:20; Romans 7:14, 17-18,23; James 3:2; 1 John 1:8,10.
12 Romans 7:5-8,25; Galatians 5:17.
13 1 John 3:4.
14 Romans 2:15; 3:9,19.
15 Ephesians 2:3.
16 Galatians 3:10.
17 Romans 6:23.
18 Ephesians 4:18.
19 Lamentations 3:39; Romans 8:20.
20 Matthew 25:41; 2 Thessalonians 1:9.

CHAPTER VII

OF GOD'S COVENANT WITH MAN.

1. The distance between God and the creature is so great, that although reasonable creatures do owe obedience to Him as their Creator, yet they could never have any fruition of Him as their blessedness and reward, except by some voluntary condescension on God's part, which He has been pleased to express by way of covenant.[1]

2. The first covenant made with man was a covenant of works,[2] in which life was promised to Adam; and in him to his descendants,[3] on condition of perfect and personal obedience.[4]

3. Man, by his fall, having made himself incapable of life by that covenant, the Lord was pleased to make a second,[5] commonly called the covenant of grace; in which He freely offers to sinners life and salvation by Jesus Christ; requiring of them faith in Him, that they may be saved,[6] and promising to give to all those who are ordained to eternal life His Holy Spirit, to make them willing, and able to believe.[7]

4. This covenant of grace is frequently set forth in Scripture by the name of a will, in reference to the death of Jesus Christ, and to the everlasting inheritance, with all things belonging to it, bequeathed in it.[8]

5. This covenant was differently administered in the time of the law, and in the time of the Gospel:[9] under the law it was administered by promises, prophecies, sacrifices, circumcision, the paschal lamb, and other types and ordinances delivered to the people of the Jews, all pointing to the Christ to come;[10] which were, for that time, sufficient and effectual, through the operation of the Spirit, to instruct and build

---

1 1 Samuel 2:25; Job 9:32-33; 22:2-3; 35:7-8; Psalms 100:2-3; 113:5-6; Isaiah 40:13-17; Luke 17:10; Acts 17:24-25.
2 Galatians 3:12.
3 Romans 5:12-20; 10:5.
4 Genesis 2:17; Galatians 3:10.
5 Genesis 3:15; Isaiah 42:6; Romans 3:20-21; 8:3; Galatians 3:21.
6 Mark 16:15-16; John 3:16; Romans 5:6-9; Galatians 3.
7 Ezekiel 36:26-27; John 6:44-45.
8 Luke 22:20; Hebrews 7:22; 9:15-17; I Corinthians 11:25.
9 2 Corinthians 3:6-9.
10 Romans 4:11; 1 Corinthians 5:7; Colossians 2:11-12; Hebrews 8; 9; 10.

up the elect in faith in the promised Messiah,[1] by whom they had full remission of sins, and eternal salvation; and is called the Old Testament.[2]

6.   Under the Gospel, when Christ, the man,[3] was exhibited, the ordinances in which this covenant is dispensed are the preaching of the Word, and the administration of the sacraments of baptism and the Lord's Supper:[4] which, though fewer in number, and administered with more simplicity, and less outward glory, yet, in them, it is held forth in more fullness, evidence, and spiritual efficacy,[5] to all peoples, both Jews and Gentiles;[6] and is called the New Testament.[7] There are not therefore two covenants of grace, differing in substance, but one and the same, under various dispensations.[8]

---

1   John 8:56; 1 Corinthians 10:1-4; Hebrews 11:13.
2   Galatians 3:7-9,14.
3   Colossians 2:17.
4   Matthew 28:19-20; 1 Corinthians 11:23-25.
5   Jeremiah 31:33-34; Hebrews 12:22-27.
6   Matthew 28:19; Ephesians 2:15-19.
7   Luke 22:20.
8   Psalm 32:1; Acts 15:11; Romans 3:21-23,30; 4:3,6,16-17,23-24; Galatians 3:14,16; Hebrews 13:8.

CHAPTER VIII

OF CHRIST THE MEDIATOR.

1. It pleased God, in His eternal purpose, to choose and ordain the Lord
    Jesus, His only begotten Son, to be the Mediator between God and
    man;[1] the Prophet,[2] Priest,[3] and King;[4] the Head and Savior of His
    Church;[5] the Heir of all things;[6] and Judge of the world:[7] to whom He
    did from all eternity give a people, to be His seed,[8] and to be by Him
    in time redeemed, called, justified, sanctified, and glorified.[9]

2. The Son of God, the second person in the Trinity, being very and
    eternal God, of one substance and equal with the Father, did, when the
    fullness of time had come, take upon Him man's nature,[10] with all the
    essential properties, and common infirmities of a man, yet without sin;[11]
    being conceived by the power of the Holy Spirit, in the womb of the
    virgin Mary, of her substance.[12] So that two whole, perfect, and distinct
    natures, the Godhead and the manhood, were inseparably joined
    together in one person, without conversion, composition, or
    confusion.[13] This person is very God, and very man, yet one Christ, the
    only Mediator between God and man.[14]

3. The Lord Jesus, in His human nature thus united to the divine, was
    sanctified, and anointed with the Holy Spirit, above measure,[15] having
    in Him all the treasures of wisdom and knowledge;[16] in whom it
    pleased the Father that all fullness should dwell;[17] to the end that, being
    holy, harmless, undefiled, and full of grace and truth,[18] He might be
    thoroughly equipped to execute the office of a Mediator and

---

1   Isaiah 42:1; John 3:16; Timothy 2:5;
    1 Peter 1:19-20.
2   Acts 3:22.
3   Hebrews 5:5-6.
4   Psalm 2:6; Luke 1:33.
5   Ephesians 5:23.
6   Hebrews 1:2.
7   Acts 17:31.
8   Psalm 22:30; Isaiah 53:10; John 17:6.
9   Isaiah 55:4-5; 1 Corinthians 1:30;
    1 Timothy 2:6.

10 John 1:1,14; Galatians 4:4; Philippians 2:6;
    1 John 5:20.
11 Hebrews 2:14,16-17; 4:15.
12 Luke 1:27,31,35; Galatians 4:4.
13 Luke 1:35; Colossians 2:9; 1 Timothy 3:16;
    1 Peter 3:18.
14 Romans 1:3-4; 1 Timothy 2:5.
15 Psalm 45:7; John 3:34.
16 Colossians 2:3.
17 Colossians 1:19.
18 John 1:14; Hebrews 7:26.

Guarantee.[1] This office He took not by Himself, but was called to it by His Father,[2] who put all power and judgment into His hand, and gave Him authority to execute the same.[3]

4.   This office the Lord Jesus did most willingly undertake;[4] so that He might discharge His duties, He was made under the law,[5] and did perfectly fulfill it.[6] He endured most grievous torments immediately in His soul,[7] and most painful sufferings in His body;[8] was crucified, and died,[9] was buried, and remained under the power of death, yet saw no decay.[10] On the third day He arose from the dead,[11] with the same body in which He suffered,[12] with which also He ascended into heaven, and there sits at the right hand of His Father,[13] making intercession,[14] and shall return, to judge men and angels, at the end of the world.[15]

5.   The Lord Jesus, by His perfect obedience and sacrifice of Himself, which He through the eternal Spirit once offered up to God, has fully satisfied the justice of His Father;[16] and purchased not only reconciliation, but an everlasting inheritance in the kingdom of heaven, for all those whom the Father has given to Him.[17]

6.   Although the work of redemption was not actually done by Christ till after His incarnation, yet the virtue, efficacy, and benefits of it were communicated to the elect, in all ages successively from the beginning of the world, in and by those promises, types, and sacrifices, through which He was revealed and shown to be the seed of the woman that should crush the serpent's head, and the Lamb slain from the beginning of the world; being yesterday and today the same, and forever.[18]

1   Hebrews 7:22; 12:24; Acts 10:38.
2   Hebrews 5:4-5.
3   Matthew 28:18; John 5:22,27; Acts 2:36.
4   Psalm 40:7-8; John 10:18; Philippians 2:8; Hebrews 10:5-10.
5   Galatians 4:4.
6   Matthew 3:15; 5:17.
7   Matthew 26:37-38; 27:46; Luke 22:44.
8   Matthew 26; 27.
9   Philippians 2:8.
10   Acts 2:23-24,27; 13:37; Romans 6:9.
11   1 Corinthians 15:3-5.
12   John 20:25,27.
13   Mark 16:19.
14   Romans 8:34; Hebrews 7:25; 9:24.
15   Matthew 13:40-42; Acts 1:11; 10:42; Romans 14:9-10; 2 Peter 2:4; Jude 6.
16   Romans 3:25-26; 5:19; Ephesians 5:2; Hebrews 9:14,16; 10:14.
17   Daniel 9:24,26; John 17:2; Ephesians 1:11,14; Colossians 1:19-20; Hebrews 9:12,15.
18   Genesis 3:15; Galatians 4:4-5; Hebrews 13:8; Revelation 13:8.

7. Christ, in the work of mediation, acts according to both natures, by each nature doing that which is proper to itself;[1] yet, by reason of the unity of the person, that which is proper to one nature is sometimes in Scripture attributed to the person denominated by the other nature.[2]

8. To all those for whom Christ has purchased redemption, He does certainly and effectually apply and communicate the same;[3] making intercession for them,[4] and revealing to them, in and by the Word, the mysteries of salvation;[5] effectually persuading them by His Spirit to believe and obey, and governing their hearts by His Word and Spirit;[6] overcoming all their enemies by His almighty power and wisdom, in such manner and ways as are most in agreement with His wonderful and unsearchable ordering of affairs.[7]

---

1   Hebrews 9:14; 1 Peter 3:18.
2   Acts 20:28; John 3:13; 1 John 3:16.
3   John 6:37,39; 10:15-16.
4   Romans 8:34; 1 John 2:1-2.
5   John 15:13,15; 17:6; Ephesians 1:7-10.
6   John 14:16; 17:17; Romans 8:9,14; 15:19-19.
7   Psalm 110:1; Malachi 4:2-3; 1 Corinthians 15:25-26; Colossians 2:15.

CHAPTER IX

OF FREE WILL.

1. God has endowed the will of man with that natural liberty, that it is neither forced, nor, by any absolute necessity of nature, determined to good, or evil. [1]

2. Man, in his state of innocence, had freedom and power to will and to do that which was good and well pleasing to God; [2] but yet, alternatively, so that he might fall from it. [3]

3. Man, by his fall into a state of sin, has wholly lost all ability of will to any spiritual good accompanying salvation: [4] so as, a natural man, being altogether averse from that good, [5] and dead in sin, [6] is not able, by his own strength, to convert himself, or to prepare himself for salvation. [7]

4. When God converts a sinner, and brings him into the state of grace, He frees him from his natural bondage under sin; [8] and, by His grace alone, enables him freely to will and to do that which is spiritually good; [9] yet so, because of his remaining corruption, he does not perfectly, nor only, will that which is good, but does also will that which is evil. [10]

5. The will of man is made perfectly and unchangeably free to do good alone in the state of glory only. [11]

1   Deuteronomy 30:19; Matthew 17:12; James 1:14.
2   Genesis 1:26; Ecclesiastes 7:29.
3   Genesis 2: 16-17; 3:6.
4   John 15:5; Romans 5:6; 8:7.
5   Romans 3:10,12.
6   Ephesians 2:1,5; Colossians 2:13.

7   John 6:44, 65; 1 Corinthians 2:14; Ephesians 2:2-5; Titus 3:3-5.
8   John 8:34,36; Colossians 1:13.
9   Romans 6:18,22; Philippians 2:13.
10   Romans 7:15, 18-19, 21,23; Galatians 5:17.
11   Ephesians 4:13; Hebrews 12:23; 1 John 3:2; Jude 24.

CHAPTER X

OF EFFECTUAL CALLING.

1. All those whom God has predestined for life, and those only, He is
    pleased, in His appointed and accepted time, effectually to call,[1] by His
    Word and Spirit,[2] out of that state of sin and death, in which they are
    by nature, to grace and salvation, by Jesus Christ;[3] enlightening their
    minds spiritually and salvifically to understand the things of God,[4]
    taking away their hearts of stone, and giving them hearts of flesh;[5]
    renewing their wills, and, by His almighty power, determining them to
    that which is good,[6] and effectually drawing them to Jesus Christ:[7] yet
    so, as they come most freely, being made willing by His grace.[8]

2. This effectual call is of God's free and special grace alone, not from
    anything at all foreseen in man,[9] who is altogether powerless in this,
    until, being quickened and renewed by the Holy Spirit,[10] he is thereby
    enabled to answer this call, and to embrace the grace offered and
    conveyed in it.[11]

3. Elect infants, dying in infancy, are regenerated, and saved by Christ,
    through the Spirit,[12] who works when, and where, and how He
    pleases:[13] so also are all other elect persons who are incapable of being
    outwardly called by the ministry of the Word.[14]

4. Others, not elected, although they may be called by the ministry of the
    Word,[15] and may have some common operations of the Spirit,[16] yet

---

1   Romans 8:30; 11:7; Ephesians 1:10-11.
2   Corinthians 3:3, 6; 2 Thessalonians 2:13-14.
3   Romans 8:2; Ephesians 2:1-5; 2 Timothy 1:9-10.
4   Acts 26:18; 1 Corinthians 2:10,12;
    Ephesians 1:17-18.
5   Ezekiel 36:26.
6   Deuteronomy 30:6; Ezekiel 11:19; 36:27;
    Philippians 2:13.
7   John 6:44-45; Ephesians 1:19.
8   Psalms 110:3; Song of Solomon 1:4; John 6:37;
    Romans 6:16-18.
9   Romans 9:11; Ephesians 2:4-5, 8-9; 2 Timothy 1:9;
    Titus 3:4-5.
10 Romans 8:7; 1 Corinthians 2:14; Ephesians 2:5.
11 John 5:25; 6:37; Ezekiel 36:27.
12 Luke 18:15-16; John 3:3,5; Acts 2:38-39;
    Romans 8:9; 1 John 5:12.
13 John 3:8.
14 Acts 4:12; 1 John 5:12.
15 Matthew 22:14.
16 Matthew 7:22; 13: 20-21; Hebrews 6:4-5.

they never truly come to Christ, and therefore cannot be saved:[1] much less can men, not professing the Christian religion, be saved in any other way whatsoever, be they ever so diligent to frame their lives according to the light of nature, and the laws of that religion they do profess.[2] And to assert and maintain that they may, is very pernicious, and to be detested.[3]

1   John 6:64-66; 8:24.
2   John 4:22; 14:6; 17:3; Acts 4:12; Ephesians 2:12.
3   1 Corinthians 16:22; Galatians 1:6-8; 2 John 9-11.

CHAPTER XI

OF JUSTIFICATION.

1. Those whom God effectually calls, He also freely justifies:[1] not by infusing righteousness in them, but by pardoning their sins, and by accounting and accepting their persons as righteous; not for anything done in them, or done by them, but for Christ's sake alone; nor by imputing faith itself, the act of believing, or any other evangelical obedience to them, as their righteousness; but by imputing the obedience and satisfaction of Christ to them,[2] they receiving and resting on Him and His righteousness by faith; which faith they have not of themselves, it is the gift of God.[3]

2. Faith, thus receiving and resting on Christ and His righteousness, is the only instrument of justification:[4] yet in the person justified it is not alone, but is ever accompanied with all other saving graces, and is no dead faith, but works by love.[5]

3. Christ, by His obedience and death, did fully discharge the debt of all those who are thus justified, and did make a proper, real, and full satisfaction to His Father's justice in their behalf.[6] Yet, in as much as He was given by the Father for them;[7] and His obedience and satisfaction accepted in their stead;[8] and both, freely, not for anything in them; their justification is only of free grace;[9] that both the exact justice, and rich grace of God might be glorified in the justification of sinners.[10]

---

1   Romans 3:24; 8:30.
2   Jeremiah 23:6; Romans 3:22,24-25,27-28; 4:5-8; 5:17-19; 1 Corinthians 1:30-31; 2 Corinthians 5:19,21; Ephesians 1:7; Titus 3:5,7.
3   Acts 10:44; 13:38-39; Galatians 2:16; Ephesians 2:7-8; Philippians 3:9.
4   John 1:12; Romans 3:28; 5:1.

5   Galatians 5:6; James 2:17,22,26.
6   Isaiah 53:4-6,10-12; Daniel 9:24,26; Romans 5:8-10,19; 1 Timothy 2:5-6; Hebrews 10:10,14.
7   Romans 8:32.
8   Matthew 3:17; Ephesians 5:2; 2 Corinthians 5:21.
9   Romans 3:24; Ephesians 1:7.
10 Romans 3:26; Ephesians 2:7.

4. God did, from all eternity, decree to justify all the elect,[1] and Christ did, in the fullness of time, die for their sins, and rise for their justification:[2] nevertheless, they are not justified, until the Holy Spirit does, in due time, actually apply Christ to them.[3]

5. God does continue to forgive the sins of those who are justified;[4] and, although they can never fall from the state of justification,[5] yet they may, by their sins, fall under God's fatherly displeasure, and not have the light of His approval restored to them, until they humble themselves, confess their sins, beg pardon, and renew their faith and repentance.[6]

6. The justification of believers under the Old Testament was, in all these respects, one and the same with the justification of believers under the New Testament.[7]

---

[1] Romans 8:30; Galatians 3:8; 1 Peter 1:2,19-20.
[2] Romans 4:25; Galatians 4:4; 1 Timothy 2:6.
[3] Galatians 2:16; Colossians 1:21-22; Titus 3:4-7.
[4] Matthew 6:12; 1 John 1:7,9; 2:1-2.
[5] Luke 22:32; John 10:28; Hebrews 10:14.
[6] Psalms 33:5; 51:7-12; 89:31-33; Matthew 26:75; Luke 1:20; 1 Corinthians 11:30,32.
[7] Romans 4:22-24; Galatians 3:9,13-14; Hebrews 13:8.

CHAPTER XII

OF ADOPTION.

1. All those who are justified, God permitted, in and for His only Son Jesus Christ, to make partakers of the grace of adoption,[1] by which they are taken into the number and enjoy the liberties and privileges of the children of God,[2] have His name put on them,[3] receive the spirit of adoption,[4] have access to the throne of grace with boldness,[5] are enabled to cry, Abba, Father,[6] are pitied,[7] protected,[8] provided for,[9] and chastened by Him as by a Father:[10] yet never cast off,[11] but sealed to the day of redemption;[12] and inherit the promises,[13] as heirs of everlasting salvation.[14]

1   Galatians 4:4-5; Ephesians 1:5.
2   John 1:12; Romans 8:17.
3   Jeremiah 14:9; 2 Corinthians 16:18; Revelation 3:12.
4   Romans 8:15.
5   Romans 5:2; Ephesians 3:12.
6   Galatians 4:6.
7   Psalms 103:13.
8   Proverbs 14:26.
9   Matthew 6:30,32; 1 Peter 5:7.
10 Hebrews 12:6.
11 Lamentations 3:31.
12 Ephesians 4:30.
13 Hebrews 6:12.
14 Hebrews 1:14; 1 Peter 1:3-4.

CHAPTER XIII

OF SANCTIFICATION.

1. They who are once effectually called, and regenerated, having a new heart, and a new spirit created in them, are further sanctified, really and personally, through the virtue of Christ's death and resurrection,[1] by His Word and Spirit dwelling in them;[2] the dominion of the whole body of sin is destroyed,[3] and the several lusts of it are more and more weakened and destroyed;[4] and they more and more made alive and strengthened in all saving graces,[5] to the practice of true holiness, without which no man shall see the Lord.[6]

2. This sanctification is throughout, in the whole man;[7] yet imperfect in this life, there remaining some remnants of corruption in every part;[8] from which arises a continual and irreconcilable war, the flesh lusting against the Spirit, and the Spirit against the flesh.[9]

3. In which war, although the remaining corruption, for a time, may much prevail;[10] yet, through the continual supply of strength from the sanctifying Spirit of Christ, the regenerate part does overcome;[11] and so, the saints grow in grace,[12] perfecting holiness in the fear of God.[13]

---

1 Acts 20:32; Romans 6:5-6; 1 Corinthians 6:11; Philippians 3:10.
2 John 17:17; Ephesians 5:26; 2 Thessalonians 2:13.
3 Romans 6:6,14.
4 Romans 8:13; Galatians 5:24.
5 Ephesians 3:16-19; Colossians 1:11.
6 2 Corinthians 7:1; Hebrews 12:14.
7 1 Thessalonians 5:23.
8 Romans 7:18,23; Philippians 3:12; 1 John 1:10.
9 Galatians 5:17; 1 Peter 2:11.
10 Romans 7:23.
11 Romans 6:14; Ephesians 4:15-16; 1 John 5:4.
12 2 Corinthians 3:18; 2 Peter 3:18.
13 2 Corinthians 7:1.

CHAPTER XIV

OF SAVING FAITH.

1.	The grace of faith, whereby the elect are enabled to believe to the saving of their souls,[1] is the work of the Spirit of Christ in their hearts,[2] and is ordinarily accomplished by the ministry of the Word,[3] by which also, and by the administration of the sacraments, and prayer, it is increased and strengthened.[4]

2.	By this faith, a Christian believes to be true whatever is revealed in the Word, for the authority of God Himself speaking in it;[5] and acts differently on that which each particular passage of it contains; yielding obedience to the commands,[6] trembling at the warnings,[7] and embracing the promises of God for this life, and that which is to come.[8] But the principal acts of saving faith are accepting, receiving, and resting on Christ alone for justification, sanctification, and eternal life, by virtue of the covenant of grace.[9]

3.	This faith is different in degrees, weak or strong;[10] may be often and many ways assailed, and weakened, but gets the victory:[11] growing up in many to the attainment of a full assurance, through Christ,[12] who is both the author and finisher of our faith.[13]

1	Hebrews 10:39.
2	2 Corinthians 4:13; Ephesians 1:17-19; 2:8.
3	Romans 10:14,17.
4	Luke 17:5; Acts 20:32; Romans 1:16-17; 4:11; 1 Peter 2:2.
5	John 4:42; Acts 24:14; 1 Thessalonians 2:13; 1 John 5:10.
6	Romans 16:26.
7	Isaiah 66:2.
8	1 Timothy 4:8; Hebrews 11:13.
9	John 1:12; Acts 15:11; 16:31; Galatians 2:20.
10	Matthew 6:30; 8:10; Romans 4:19-20; Hebrews 5:13-14.
11	Luke 22:31-32; Ephesians 6:16; 1 John 5:4-5.
12	Hebrews 6:11-12; 10:22.
13	Hebrews 12:2.

CHAPTER XV

OF REPENTANCE TO LIFE.

1. Repentance to life is an evangelical grace,[1] the doctrine of which is to be preached by every minister of the Gospel, as well as the doctrine of faith in Christ.[2]

2. By it, a sinner, because of the sight and sense not only of the danger, but also of the filthiness and odiousness of his sins, as contrary to the holy nature, and righteous law of God; and upon the understanding of His mercy in Christ to such as are penitent, so grieves for, and hates his sins, as to turn from them all to God,[3] intending and endeavoring to walk with Him in all the ways of His commandments.[4]

3. Although repentance is not to be rested in, as any satisfaction for sin, or any cause of the pardon for it,[5] which is the act of God's free grace in Christ;[6] yet it is of such necessity to all sinners, that none may expect pardon without it.[7]

4. As there is no sin so small, but it deserves damnation;[8] so there is no sin so great, that it can bring damnation on those who truly repent.[9]

5. Men ought not to be content with a general repentance, but it is every man's duty to endeavor to repent of his individual sins, individually.[10]

6. As every man is bound to make private confession of his sins to God, praying for the pardon of them;[11] upon which, and the forsaking of them, he shall find mercy;[12] so, he who brings scandal on his brother, or the Church of Christ, ought to be willing, by a private or public confession, and sorrow for his sin, to declare his repentance to those who are offended,[13] who are then to be reconciled to him, and in love to receive him.[14]

---

1 Zechariah 12:10; Acts 11:18.
2 Mark 1:15; Luke 24:47; Acts 20:21.
3 Psalms 51:4; 119:128; Isaiah 30:22; Jeremiah 31:18-19; Ezekiel 18:30-31; 36:31; Joel 2:12-13,15; Amos 15; 2 Corinthians 7:11.
4 2 Kings 23:25; Psalms 119:6,59,106; Luke 1:6.
5 Ezekiel 16:61-63; 36:31-32.
6 Hosea 14:2,4; Romans 3:24; Ephesians 1:7.
7 Luke 13:3,5; Acts 17:30-31.
8 Matthew 12:36; Romans 5:12; 6:23.
9 Isaiah 1:16,18; 55:7; Romans 8:1.
10 Psalms 19:13; Luke 19:8; 1 Timothy 1:13,15.
11 Psalms 32:5-6; 51:4-5,7,9,14.
12 Proverbs 28:13; 1 John 1:9.
13 Joshua 7:19; Psalms 51; Luke 17:3-4; James 5:16.
14 2 Corinthians 2:8.

CHAPTER XVI

OF GOOD WORKS.

1. Good works are only such as God has commanded in His holy Word,[1] and not such as, without the warrant of Scripture, are devised by men, out of blind zeal, or on any pretense of good intention.[2]

2. These good works, done in obedience to God's commandments, are the fruits and evidences of a true and living faith:[3] and by them believers show their thankfulness,[4] strengthen their assurance,[5] teach their brothers,[6] give credibility to their profession of the Gospel,[7] stop the criticism from the adversaries,[8] and glorify God,[9] whose workmanship they are, created in Christ Jesus for such purpose,[10] that, having their fruit of holiness, they may have the end, eternal life.[11]

3. Their ability to do good works is not at all of themselves, but wholly from the Spirit of Christ.[12] And that they may be enabled to do so, besides the graces they have already received, there is required an actual influence of the same Holy Spirit to work in them to will, and to do, of His good pleasure:[13] yet they are not in this to grow negligent, as if they were not bound to perform any duty unless on a special motion of the Spirit; but they ought to be diligent in stirring up the grace of God that is in them.[14]

4. They who, in their obedience, attain to the greatest height that is possible in this life, are so far from being able to do more than God requires, that they fall short of much which in duty they are bound to do.[15]

1   Micah 6:8; Romans 12:2; Hebrews 13:21.
2   1 Samuel 15:21-23; Isaiah 29:13; Matthew 15:9; John 16:2; Romans 10:2; 1 Peter 1:18.
3   James 2:18, 22.
4   Psalms 116:12-13; 1 Peter 2:9.
5   2 Peter 1:5-10; 1 John 2:3,5.
6   Matthew 5:16; 2 Corinthians 9:2.
7   1 Timothy 6:1; Titus 2:5, 9-12.
8   1 Peter 2:15.
9   John 15:8; Philippians 1:11; 1 Peter 2:12.
10 Ephesians 2:10.
11 Romans 6:22.
12 Ezekiel 36:26-27; John 15:4-6.
13 2 Corinthians 3:5; Philippians 2:13; 4:13.
14 Isaiah 64:7; Acts 26:6-7; Philippians 2:12; 2 Timothy 1:6; Hebrews 6:11-12; 2 Peter 1:3,5,10-11; Jude 20-21.
15 Nehemiah 13:22; Job 9:2-3; Luke 17:10; Galatians 5:17.

5. We cannot by our best works merit pardon of sin, or eternal life in the presence of God, by reason of the great separation that is between them and the glory to come; and the infinite distance that is between us and God, whom, by our works, we can neither profit, nor satisfy for the debt of our former sins,[1] but when we have done all we can, we have done but our duty, and are unworthy servants:[2] and because, as they are good, they proceed from His Spirit;[3] and as they are done by us, they are defiled, and mixed with so much weakness and imperfection, that they cannot endure the severity of God's judgment.[4]

6. Notwithstanding, the persons of believers being accepted through Christ, their good works also are accepted in Him;[5] not as though they were in this life wholly undeserving of blame and punishment in God's sight;[6] but that He, looking on them in His Son, is pleased to accept and reward that which is sincere, although accompanied with many weaknesses and imperfections.[7]

7. Works done by unregenerate men, although at the center of them they may be things which God commands; and of good use both to themselves and others:[8] yet, because they proceed not from a heart purified by faith;[9] nor are done in a right manner, according to the Word;[10] nor to a right end, the glory of God,[11] they are therefore sinful, and cannot please God, or make a man fit to receive grace from God:[12] and yet, their neglect of them is more sinful and displeasing to God.[13]

---

1 Job 22:2-3; 35:7-8; Psalms 16:2; Romans 3:20; 4:2,4,6; 8:18; Ephesians 2:8-9; Titus 3:5-7.
2 Luke 17:10.
3 Galatians 5:22-23.
4 Psalms 130:3; 143:2; Isaiah 64:6; Romans 7:15,18; Galatians 5:17.
5 Genesis 4:4; Exodus 28:38; Ephesians 1:6; Hebrews 11:4; 1 Peter 2:5.
6 Job 9:20; Psalms 143:2.
7 Matthew 25:21,23; Hebrews 6:10; 13:20-21; 2 Corinthians 8:12.
8 1 Kings 21:27,29; 2 Kings 10:30-31; Philippians 1:15-16,18.
9 Genesis 4:5; Hebrews 11:4,6.
10 Isaiah 1:12; 1 Corinthians 13:3.
11 Matthew 6:2,5,16.
12 Hosea 1:4; Amos 5:21-22; Haggai 2:14; Romans 9:16; Titus 1:15; 3:5.
13 Job 21:14-15; Psalms 14:4; 36:3; Matthew 23:23; 25:41-43,45.

CHAPTER XVII

OF THE PERSEVERANCE OF THE SAINTS.

1.   They, whom God has accepted in His Beloved, effectually called, and sanctified by His Spirit, can neither totally nor finally fall away from the state of grace, but shall certainly persevere in grace to the end, and be eternally saved.[1]

2.   This perseverance of the saints depends not on their own free will, but on the unchangeableness of the decree of election, flowing from the free and unchangeable love of God the Father;[2] upon the efficacy of the merit and intercession of Jesus Christ,[3] the remaining of the Spirit, and of the seed of God within them,[4] and the nature of the covenant of grace:[5] from all of which arise also the certainty and infallibility of it.[6]

3.   Nevertheless, they may, through the temptations of Satan and of the world, the prevalence of corruption remaining in them, and the neglect of the means of their preservation, fall into grievous sins;[7] and, for a time, continue in them:[8] whereby they incur God's displeasure,[9] and grieve His Holy Spirit,[10] come to be deprived of some measure of their graces and comforts,[11] have their hearts hardened,[12] and their consciences wounded;[13] hurt and scandalize others,[14] and bring temporal judgments on themselves.[15]

---

1   Philippians 1:6; 1 Peter 1:5,9; 2 Peter 1:10; 1 John 3:9.
2   Jeremiah 31:3; 2 Timothy 2:18-19.
3   Luke 22:32; John 17:11,24; Romans 8:33-39; Hebrews 7:25; 9:12-15; 10:10,14; 13:20-21.
4   John 14:16-17; 1 John 2:27; 3:9.
5   Jeremiah 32:40.
6   John 10:28; 2 Thessalonians 3:3; 1 John 2:19.
7   Matthew 26:70,72,74.
8   Psalms 51.
9   2 Samuel 11:27; Isaiah 64:5,7,9.
10   Ephesians 4:30.
11   Psalms 51:8,10,12; Song of Solomon 5:2-4,6; Revelation 2:4.
12   Isaiah 63:17; Mark 6:52; 16:14.
13   Psalms 32:3-4; 51:8.
14   2 Samuel 12:14.
15   Psalms 89:31-32; 1 Corinthians 11:32.

CHAPTER XVIII

OF ASSURANCE OF GRACE AND SALVATION.

1. Although hypocrites and other unregenerate men may vainly deceive themselves with false hopes and worldly presumptions of being in the favor of God, and estate of salvation[1] (the hope of which shall perish):[2] yet such as truly believe in the Lord Jesus, and love Him in sincerity, endeavoring to walk in all good conscience before Him, may, in this life, be certainly assured that they are in the state of grace,[3] and may rejoice in the hope of the glory of God, which hope shall never make them ashamed.[4]

2. This certainty is not merely conjecture and probable conclusion grounded on a fallible hope;[5] but an infallible assurance of faith founded on the divine truth of the promises of salvation,[6] the inward evidence of those graces on which these promises are made,[7] the testimony of the Spirit of adoption witnessing with our spirits that we are the children of God,[8] which Spirit is the deposit on our inheritance, by which we are sealed to the day of redemption.[9]

3. This infallible assurance does not so belong to the essence of faith, but that a true believer may wait long, and conflict with many difficulties, before he have it:[10] yet, being enabled by the Spirit to know the things that are freely given him of God, he may, without extraordinary revelation in the right use of ordinary means, attain to it.[11] And therefore

---

1   Deuteronomy 29:19; Job 8:13-14; Micah 3:11; John 8:41.
2   Matthew 7:22-23.
3   1 John 2:3; 3:14,18-19,21,24; 5:13.
4   Romans 5:2,5.
5   Hebrews 6:11,19.
6   Hebrews 6:17-18.
7   2 Corinthians 1:12; 2 Peter 1:4-5,10-11; 1 John 2:3; 3:14.
8   Romans 8:15-16.
9   2 Corinthians 1:21-22; Ephesians 1:13-14; 4:30.
10 Psalms 77:1-12; 88; Isaiah 50:10; Mark 9:24; 1 John 5:13.
11 1 Corinthians 2:12; Ephesians 3:17; Hebrews 6:11-12; 1 John 4:13.

it is the duty of everyone to give all diligence to make his calling and election sure,[1] that thereby his heart may be enlarged in peace and joy in the Holy Spirit, in love and thankfulness to God, and in strength and cheerfulness in the duties of obedience,[2] the proper fruits of this assurance; so far is it from inclining men to indifference.[3]

4. True believers may have the assurance of their salvation shaken in many ways, diminished, and interrupted; as, by negligence in preserving of it, by falling into some special sin that wounds the conscience and grieves the Spirit; by some sudden or vehement temptation, by God's withdrawing the light of His approval, and permitting even those who fear Him to walk in darkness and to have no light:[4] yet are they never utterly destitute of that seed of God, and life of faith, that love of Christ and the brothers, that sincerity of heart, and conscience of duty, out of which, by the operation of the Spirit, this assurance may, in due time, be revived;[5] and be that which, in the meantime, they are supported from utter despair.[6]

1   2 Peter 1:10.
2   Psalms 4:6-7; 119; 32; Romans 5:1-2,5; 14:17; 15:13; Ephesians 1:3-4.
3   Psalms 130:4; Romans 6:1-2; 8:1,12; 2 Corinthians 7:1; Titus 2:11-12,14; 1 John 1:6-7; 2:1-2; 3:2-3.
4   Psalms 31:22; 51:8,12,14; 77:1-10; 88; Song of Solomon 5:2,3,6; Isaiah 50:10; Matthew 26:69-72; Ephesians 4:30,31.
5   Job 13:15; Psalms 51:8,12: 73:15; Isaiah 50:10; Luke 22:32; 1 John 3:9.
6   Psalms 22:1; 88; Isaiah 54:7-10; Jeremiah 32:40; Micah 7:7-9.

CHAPTER XIX

OF THE LAW OF GOD.

1. God gave to Adam a law, as a covenant of works, by which He bound him and all his posterity, to personal, entire, exact, and perpetual obedience, promised life upon the fulfilling, and threatened death upon the breach of it, and provided him with power and ability to keep it.[1]

2. This law, after his fall, continued to be a perfect rule of righteousness; and, as such, was delivered by God on Mount Sinai, in ten commandments, and written in two tables:[2] the first four commandments containing our duty toward God; and the other six, our duty toward man.[3]

3. Besides this law, commonly called moral, God was pleased to give to the people of Israel, as a church not yet mature, ceremonial laws, containing several typical ordinances, partly of worship, prefiguring Christ, His graces, actions, sufferings, and benefits;[4] and partly, holding forth various instructions of moral duties.[5] All of these ceremonial laws are now abrogated, under the New Testament.[6]

4. To them also, as a nation, He gave many judicial laws, which expired together with the state of that people; not obliging any other now, further than the general equity of them may require.[7]

5. The moral law does forever bind all, justified persons as well as others, to the obedience of it;[8] and that, not only in regard to the matter contained in it, but also in respect of the authority of God the Creator, who gave it.[9] Neither does Christ, in the Gospel, any way dissolve, but much strengthen this obligation.[10]

---

1   Genesis 1:26-27; 2:17; Job 28:28;
    Ecclesiastes 7:29; Romans 2:14-15; 5:12,19; 10:5;
    Galatians 3:10,12.
2   Exodus 34:1; Deuteronomy 5:32; 10:4;
    Romans 13:8-9; James 1:25; 2:8,10-12.
3   Matthew 22:37-40.
4   Galatians 9:1-3; Colossians 2:17; Hebrews 9; 10:1.
5   1 Corinthians 5:7; 2 Corinthians 6:17; Jude 23.
6   Daniel 9:27; Ephesians 2:15-16;
    Colossians 2:14,16,17.
7   Genesis 49:10; Exodus 21; Exodus 22:1-29;
    Matthew 5:17, 38-39; 1 Corinthians 9:8-10;
    1 Peter 2:13-14.
8   Romans 13:8, 9; Ephesians 6:2; 1 John 2:3-4 ,7-8.
9   James 2:10,11.
10 Matthew 5:17-19; Romans 3:31; James 2:8.

6.   Although true believers are not under the law, as a covenant of works, to be justified, or condemned by it;[1] yet is it of great use to them, as well as to others; in that, as a rule of life informing them of the will of God, and their duty, it directs and binds them to walk accordingly;[2] discovering also the sinful pollutions of their nature, hearts, and lives;[3] so as, examining themselves thereby, they may come to further conviction of, humiliation for, and hatred against sin,[4] together with a clearer sight of the need they have of Christ, and the perfection of His obedience.[5] It is likewise of use to the regenerate, to restrain their corruptions, in that it forbids sin:[6] and the warnings of it serve to show what even their sins deserve; and what afflictions, in this life, they may expect for them, although freed from the curse threatened in the law.[7] The promises of it, in like manner, show them God's approval of obedience, and what blessings they may expect for the performance of it:[8] although not as due to them by the law as a covenant of works.[9] So as, a man's doing good, and refraining from evil, because the law encourages to the one, and deters from the other, is no evidence of his being under the law; and not under grace.[10]

7.   Neither are these uses of the law contrary to the grace of the Gospel, but do sweetly comply with it;[11] the Spirit of Christ subduing and enabling the will of man to do that freely, and cheerfully, which the will of God, revealed in the law, requires to be done.[12]

1   Acts 13:39; Romans 6:14; 8:1;
    Galatians 2:16; 3:13; 4:4-5.
2   Psalms 119:4-6; Romans 7:12,22,25;
    1 Corinthians 7:19;
    Galatians 5:14,16,18-23.
3   Romans 3:20; 7:7.
4   Romans 7:9,14,24; James 1:23-25.
5   Romans 7:24; 8:3-4; Galatians 3:24.
6   Psalms 119:101,104,128; James 2:11.

7   Ezra 9:13-14; Psalms 84:30-34.
8   Leviticus 26:1-14; Psalms 19:11; 37:11;
    Matthew 5:5; 2 Corinthians 6:16; Ephesians 6:2-3.
9   Luke 17:10; Galatians 2:16.
10   Psalms 34:12-16; Romans 6:12,14;
    Hebrews 12:28-29; 1 Peter 3:8-12.
11   Galatians 3:21.
12   Jeremiah 31:33; Ezekiel 36:27; Hebrews 8:10.

CHAPTER XX

OF CHRISTIAN LIBERTY,
AND LIBERTY OF CONSCIENCE.

1.   The liberty that Christ has purchased for believers under the Gospel
     consists in their freedom from the guilt of sin, the condemning wrath of
     God, the curse of the moral law;[1] and, in their being delivered from this
     present evil world, bondage to Satan, and dominion of sin;[2] from the
     evil of afflictions, the sting of death, the victory of the grave, and
     everlasting damnation;[3] as also, in their free access to God,[4] and their
     yielding obedience to Him, not out of slavish fear, but a child-like love
     and willing mind.[5] All these were common also to believers under the
     law.[6] But, under the New Testament, the liberty of Christians is further
     enlarged, in their freedom from the yoke of the ceremonial law, to
     which the Jewish church was subjected;[7] and in greater boldness of
     access to the throne of grace,[8] and in fuller communications of the free
     Spirit of God, than believers under the law did ordinarily have.[9]
2.   God alone is Lord of the conscience,[10] and has left it free from the
     doctrines and commandments of men, which are, in anything, contrary
     to His Word; or besides it, if matters of faith, or worship.[11] So that, to
     believe such doctrines, or to obey such commands, out of conscience,
     is to betray true liberty of conscience:[12] and the requiring of an implicit

---

1   Galatians 3:13; 1 Thessalonians 1:10; Titus 2:14.
2   Acts 26:18; Romans 6:14; Galatians 1:4;
    Colossians 1:13.
3   Psalms 119:71; Romans 8:1; 8:28;
    1 Corinthians 15:54-57.
4   Romans 5:1-2.
5   Romans 8:14-15; 1 John 4:18.
6   1 Corinthians 5:7; Galatians 3:9,14,11.
7   Acts 15:10-11; Galatians 4:1-3,6-7; 5:1.
8   Hebrews 4:14,16; 10:19-22.
9   John 7:38-39; 2 Corinthians 3:13,17-18.
10 Romans 14:4; James 4:12.
11 Matthew 15:9; 23:8-10; Acts 4:19; 5:29;
    1 Corinthians 7:23; 2 Corinthians 2:24.
12 Galatians 1:10; 2:4-5; 5:1; Colossians 2:20,22-23.

faith, and an absolute and blind obedience, is to destroy liberty of conscience, and reason also.[1]

3. They who, upon pretense of Christian liberty, do practice any sin, or cherish any lust, do thereby destroy the end of Christian liberty, which is, that being delivered out of the hands of our enemies, we might serve the Lord without fear, in holiness and righteousness before Him, all the days of our lives.[2]

4. And because the powers which God has ordained, and the liberty that Christ has purchased, are not intended by God to destroy, but mutually to uphold and preserve one another, they who, upon pretense of Christian liberty, shall oppose any lawful power, or the lawful exercise of it, whether it be civil or ecclesiastical, resist the ordinance of God.[3] And, for their publishing of such opinions, or maintaining of such practices, as are contrary to the light of nature, or to the known principles of Christianity (whether concerning faith, worship, or conversation), or to the power of godliness; or, such erroneous opinions or practices, as either in their own nature, or in the manner of publishing or maintaining them, are destructive to the external peace and order which Christ has established in the Church, they may lawfully be called to account.[4]

---

1   Isaiah 8:20; Jeremiah 8:9; Hosea 5:11; John 4:22; Acts 17:11; Romans 10:17; 14:23; Revelation 13:12, 16-17.
2   Luke 1:74-75; John 8:34; Galatians 5:13; 1 Peter 2:16; 2 Peter 2:19.
3   Matthew 12:25; Romans 13:1-8; Hebrews 13:17; 1 Peter 2:13-14,16.
4   Matthew 18:15-17; Romans 1:32; 1 Corinthians 5:1,5,11,13;
    2 Thessalonians 3:14; 1 Timothy 1:19-20; 6:3-5; Titus 1:10-11,13; 3:10; Revelation 2:2,14-15,20; 3:9.

CHAPTER XXI

OF RELIGIOUS WORSHIP, AND THE SABBATH DAY.

1. The light of nature shows that there is a God, who has lordship and sovereignty over all, is good, and does good to all, and is therefore to be feared, loved, praised, called upon, trusted in, and served, with all the heart, and with all the soul, and with all the might.[1] But the acceptable way of worshipping the true God is instituted by Him, and so limited by His own revealed will, that He may not be worshipped according to the imaginations and devices of men, or the suggestions of Satan, under any visible representation, or any other way not prescribed in the Holy Scripture.[2]

2. Religious worship is to be given to God, the Father, Son, and Holy Spirit; and to Him alone;[3] not to angels, saints, or any other creature:[4] and, since the fall, not without a Mediator; nor in the mediation of any other but of Christ alone.[5]

3. Prayer, with thanksgiving, being one special part of religious worship,[6] is by God required of all men:[7] and, that it may be accepted, it is to be made in the name of the Son,[8] by the help of His Spirit,[9] according to His will,[10] with understanding, reverence, humility, passion, faith, love, and perseverance;[11] and, if vocal, in a known tongue.[12]

---

1   Joshua 24:14; Psalms 18:3; 31:23; 62:8; 119:68; Jeremiah 10:7; Mark 12:33; Acts 17:24; Romans 1:20; 10:12.
2   Exodus 20:4-6; Deuteronomy 12:32; 15:1-20; Matthew 9:9-10; 15:9; Acts 17:25; Colossians 2:23.
3   Matthew 4:10; John 5:23; 2 Corinthians 13:14.
4   Romans 1:25; Colossians 2:18; Revelation 19:10.
5   John 14:6; Ephesians 2:18; Colossians 3:17; 1 Timothy 2:5.
6   Philippians 4:6.
7   Psalms 65:2.
8   John 14:13-14; 1 Peter 2:5.
9   Romans 8:26.
10 1 John 5:14.
11 Genesis 18:27; Psalms 47:7; Ecclesiastes 5:1-2; Matthew 6:12,14-15; Mark 11:24; Ephesians 6:18; Colossians 4:2; Hebrews 12:28; James 1:6-7; 5:16.
12 1 Corinthians 14:14.

4.   Prayer is to be made for things lawful;[1] and for all sorts of men living, or who shall live hereafter:[2] but not for the dead,[3] nor for those of whom it may be known that they have sinned the sin that leads to death.[4]

5.   The reading of the Scriptures with godly fear,[5] the sound preaching[6] and conscientious hearing of the Word, in obedience to God, with understanding, faith and reverence,[7] singing of psalms with grace in the heart;[8] as also, the due administration and worthy receiving of the sacraments instituted by Christ, are all parts of the ordinary religious worship of God:[9] besides religious oaths,[10] vows,[11] solemn fasting,[12] and thanksgiving on special occasions,[13] which are, in their various times and seasons, to be used in a holy and religious manner.[14]

6.   Neither prayer, nor any other part of religious worship, is now, under the Gospel, either tied to, or made more acceptable by any place in which it is performed, or toward which it is directed:[15] but God is to be worshipped everywhere,[16] in spirit and truth;[17] as, in private families[18] daily,[19] and in secret, each one by himself;[20] so, more solemnly in the public assemblies, which are not carelessly or willfully to be neglected, or forsaken, when God, by His Word or providence, so calls.[21]

7.   As it is the law of nature, that, in general, a due proportion of time be set apart for the worship of God; so, in His Word, by a positive, moral, and perpetual commandment binding all men in all ages, He has particularly appointed one day in seven, for a Sabbath, to be kept holy to him:[22] which, from the beginning of the world to the resurrection of

1   1 John 5:14.
2   Ruth 4:12; 2 Samuel 7:29; John 17:20; 1 Timothy 2:1-2.
3   2 Samuel 12:21-23; Luke 16:25-26; Revelation 14:13.
4   1 John 5:16.
5   Acts 15:21; Revelation 1:3.
6   2 Timothy 4:2.
7   Isaiah 66:2; Matthew 13:19; Acts 10:33; Hebrews 4:2; James 1:22.
8   Ephesians 5:19,13; Colossians 3:16; James 5:13.
9   Matthew 28:19; Acts 2:42; 1 Corinthians 11:23-29.
10 Deuteronomy 6:13; Nehemiah 10:29.
11 Ecclesiastes 5:4-5; Isaiah 19:21.
12 Esther 4:16; Joel 2:12; Matthew 9:15; 1 Corinthians 7:5.
13 Esther 9:22; Psalms 107.
14 Hebrews 12:28.
15 John 4:21.
16 Malachi 1:11; 1 Timothy 2:8.
17 John 4:23-24.
18 Deuteronomy 6:6-7; 2 Samuel 6:18,20; Job 1:5; Jeremiah 10:25; Acts 10:2; 1 Peter 3:7.
19 Matthew 6:11.
20 Matthew 6:6; Ephesians 6:18.
21 Proverbs 1:20-21,24; 8:34; Isaiah 56:6-7; Luke 4:16; Acts 2:42; 13:42; Hebrews 10:25.
22 Exodus 20:8,10-11; Isaiah 56:2,4,6-7.

Christ, was the last day of the week; and, from the resurrection of Christ, was changed into the first day of the week,[1] which, in Scripture, is called the Lord's Day,[2] and is to be continued to the end of the world, as the Christian Sabbath.[3]

8.   This Sabbath is then kept holy to the Lord, when men, after a due preparing of their hearts, and ordering of their common affairs beforehand, do not only observe a holy rest all the day from their own works, words, and thoughts about their worldly employments and recreations,[4] but also are taken up, the whole time, in the public and private exercises of His worship, and in the duties of necessity and mercy.[5]

1   Genesis 2:2-3; Acts 20:7; 1 Corinthians 16:1.
2   Revelation 1:10.
3   Exodus 20:8,10; Matthew 5:17-18.
4   Exodus 16:23,25-26,29-30; 20:8; 31:15-17; Nehemiah 13:15-19,21-22; Isaiah 58:13.
5   Isaiah 58:13; Matthew 12:1-13.

CHAPTER XXII

OF LAWFUL OATHS AND VOWS.

1. A lawful oath is part of religious worship,[1] in which, on an appropriate occasion, the person swearing solemnly calls God to witness what he asserts, or promises, and to judge him according to the truth or falsehood of what he swears.[2]

2. The name of God only is that by which men ought to swear, and it is to be used with all holy fear and reverence.[3] Therefore, to swear vainly, or rashly, by that glorious and dreadful Name; or, to swear at all by any other thing, is sinful, and to be abhorred.[4] Yet, as in matters of weight and moment, an oath is warranted by the Word of God, under the New Testament as well as under the old;[5] so a lawful oath, being imposed by lawful authority, in such matters, ought to be taken.[6]

3. Whoever takes an oath ought to consider the weightiness of so solemn an act, and in it to declare nothing but what he is fully convinced is the truth:[7] neither may any man bind himself by oath to anything but what is good and just, and what he believes to be so, and what he is able and resolved to perform.[8,9]

4. An oath is to be taken in the plain and common sense of the words, without equivocation, or mental reservation.[10] It cannot oblige to sin; but in anything not sinful, being taken, it binds to performance, even though it may hurt the one making the oath.[11] Nor is it to be violated, although made to heretics, or unbelievers.[12]

5. A vow is like a promissory oath, and ought to be made with similar religious care, and to be performed with the same faithfulness.[13]

---

1   Deuteronomy 10:20.
2   Exodus 20:7; Leviticus 19:12; 2 Corinthians 1:23; 6:22-23.
3   Deuteronomy 6:13.
4   Exodus 20:7; Jeremiah 5:7; Matthew 5:34, 37; James 5:12.
5   Isaiah 65:16; 2 Corinthians 1:23; Hebrews 6:16.
6   1 Kings 8:31; Ezra 10:5; Nehemiah 13:25.
7   Exodus 20:7; Jeremiah 4:2.
8   Genesis 24:2-3,5-6,8-9.
9   Intentionally omitted
10 Psalms 24:4; Jeremiah 4:2.
11 1 Samuel 25:22,32-34; Psalms 15:4.
12 Joshua 9:18-19; 2 Samuel 21:1; Ezekiel 17:16, 18-19.
13 Psalms 61:8; 66:13-14; Ecclesiastes 5:4-6; Isaiah 19:21.

6. It is not to be made to any creature, but to God alone:[1] and, that it may be accepted, it is to be made voluntarily, out of faith, and conscience of duty, in way of thankfulness for mercy received, or for the obtaining of what we want, whereby we more strictly bind ourselves to necessary duties: or, to other things, so far and so long as they may aptly contribute to the intended result.[2]

7. No man may vow to do anything forbidden in the Word of God, or what would hinder any duty commanded in it, or which is not in his own power, and for the performance of which he has no promise of ability from God.[3] In which respects, Roman Catholic monastical vows of perpetual single life, professed poverty, and regular obedience, are so far from being degrees of higher perfection, that they are superstitious and sinful snares, in which no Christian may entangle himself.[4]

---

1   Psalms 76:11; Jeremiah 44:25-26.
2   Genesis 28:20-22; Deuteronomy 23:21-23; 1 Samuel 1:11; Psalms 50:14; 66:13-14; 132:2-5.
3   Numbers 30:5,8,12-13; Mark 6:26; Acts 23:12,14.
4   Matthew 19:11-12; 1 Corinthians 7:2,9; 7:23; Ephesians 4:28; 1 Peter 4:2.

CHAPTER XXIII

OF THE CIVIL MAGISTRATE.

1. God, the supreme Lord and King of all the world, has ordained civil magistrates to be under Him, over the people, for His own glory, and the public good: and, to this end, has armed them with the power of the sword, for the defense and encouragement of those who are good, and for the punishment of evildoers.[1]

2. It is lawful for Christians to accept and execute the office of a magistrate, when so called:[2] in the managing of it, as they ought especially to maintain piety, justice, and peace, according to the wholesome laws of each commonwealth;[3] so, for that end, they may lawfully, now under the New Testament, wage war, upon just and necessary occasion.[4]

3. Civil magistrates may not assume to themselves the administration of the Word and sacraments;[5] or the power of the keys of the kingdom of heaven;[6] or, in the least, interfere in the matters of faith.[7] Yet, as nursing fathers, it is the duty of civil magistrates to protect the Church of our common Lord, without giving the preference to any denomination of Christians above the rest, in such a manner that all ecclesiastical persons whatever shall enjoy the full, free, and unquestioned liberty of discharging every part of their sacred functions, without violence or danger.[8] And, as Jesus Christ has appointed a regular government and discipline in His Church, no law of any commonwealth should interfere with, let, or hinder, the due exercise thereof, among the voluntary members of any denomination of Christians, according to their own

---

1   Romans 13:1-4; 1 Peter 2:13-14.

2   Proverbs 8:15-16; Romans 13:1-2,4.

3   2 Samuel 23:3; Psalms 2:10-12; 82:3-4; 1 Timothy 2:2; 1 Peter 2:13.

4   Matthew 8:9-10; Luke 3:14; Acts 10:1-2; Romans 13:4; Revelation 17:14,16.

5   2 Chronicles 26:18.

6   Matthew 16:19; 18:17; Romans 10:15; 1 Corinthians 4:1-2; 12:28-29; Ephesians 4:11-12; Hebrews 5:4.

7   John 18:36; Acts 5:29; Ephesians 4:11-12.

8   Isaiah 49:23; Romans 13:1-6.

profession and belief.[1] It is the duty of civil magistrates to protect the person and good name of all their people, in such an effectual manner that no person be permitted, either upon pretense of religion or of infidelity, to offer any indignity, violence, abuse, or injury to any other person whatsoever: and to take order, that all religious and ecclesiastical assemblies be held without molestation or disturbance.[2]

4. It is the duty of people to pray for magistrates,[3] to honor their persons,[4] to pay them tribute or other dues,[5] to obey their lawful commands, and to be subject to their authority, for conscience's sake.[6] Infidelity, or difference in religion, does not make void the magistrates' just and legal authority, nor free the people from their due obedience to them:[7] from which ecclesiastical persons are not exempted,[8] much less has the pope any power and jurisdiction over them in their dominions, or over any of their people; and, least of all, to deprive them of their dominions, or lives, if he shall judge them to be heretics, or upon any other pretense whatever.[9]

1   Psalms 105:15; Acts 18:14-15.
2   Romans 13:4; 1 Timothy 2:2.
3   1 Timothy 2:1-2.
4   1 Peter 2:17.
5   Romans 13:6-7.
6   Romans 13:5; Titus 3:1.
7   1 Peter 2:13-14,16.
8   1 Kings 2:35; Acts 25:9-11; Romans 13:1; 2 Peter 2:1,10-11; Jude 8-11,
9   2 Thessalonians 2:4; Revelation 13:15-17.

CHAPTER XXIV

OF MARRIAGE AND DIVORCE.

1. Marriage is to be between one man and one woman: neither is it lawful for any man to have more than one wife, nor for any woman to have more than one husband, at the same time.[1]

2. Marriage was ordained for the mutual help of husband and wife,[2] for the increase of mankind with legitimate descendants, and of the Church with a holy seed;[3] and for preventing of uncleanness.[4]

3. It is lawful for all sorts of people to marry, who are able with judgment to give their consent.[5] Yet it is the duty of Christians to marry only in the Lord.[6] And therefore such as profess the true reformed religion should not marry with infidels, papists, or other idolaters: neither should such as are godly be unequally yoked, by marrying with such as are notoriously wicked in their lives, or maintain damnable heresies.[7]

4. Marriage ought not to be within the degrees of blood relationship or family closeness forbidden by the Word.[8] Nor can such incestuous marriage ever be made by any law of man or consent of parties, so as those persons may live together as man and wife.[9]

5. Adultery or fornication committed after entering into a contract, being detected before marriage, give just occasion to the innocent party to dissolve that contract.[10] In the case of adultery after marriage, it is lawful for the innocent party to sue out a divorce,[11] and, after the divorce, to marry another, as if the offending party were dead.[12]

1   Genesis 2:24; Proverbs 2:17; Matthew 19:5-6.
2   Genesis 2:18.
3   Malachi 2:15.
4   1 Corinthians 7:2,9.
5   1 Corinthians 7:36-38; 1 Timothy 4:3; Hebrews 13:4.
6   1 Corinthians 7:39.
7   Genesis 34:14; Exodus 34:16; Deuteronomy 7:3-4; 1 Kings 11:4; Nehemiah 13:25-27; Malachi 2:11-12; 2 Corinthians 6:14.
8   Leviticus 18; Amos 2:7; 1 Corinthians 5:1.
9   Leviticus 18:24-28; Mark 6:18.
10 Matthew 1:18-20.
11 Matthew 5:31-32.
12 Matthew 19:9; Romans 7:2-3.

6. Although the corruption of man be such that he is apt to study arguments unduly to separate those whom God has joined together in marriage: yet, nothing but adultery, or such willful desertion as can no way be remedied by the Church, or civil magistrate, is sufficient cause for dissolving the bond of marriage:[1] in this, a public and orderly course of proceeding is to be observed; and the persons concerned in it not left to their own wills and discretion in their own case.[2]

1   Matthew 19:8-9; 19:6; 1 Corinthians 7:15.
2   Deuteronomy 24:1-4.

CHAPTER XXV

OF THE CHURCH.

1. The catholic or universal Church, which is invisible, consists of the whole number of the elect, who have been, are, or shall be gathered into one, under Christ its Head; and is the spouse, the body, the fullness of Him who fills everything in every way.[1]

2. The visible Church, which is also catholic or universal under the Gospel (not confined to one nation, as before under the law), consists of all those throughout the world who profess the true religion;[2] and of their children:[3] and is the kingdom of the Lord Jesus Christ,[4] the house and family of God,[5] out of which there is no ordinary possibility of salvation.[6]

3. To this catholic visible Church, Christ has given the ministry, Scriptures, and means of grace of God, for the gathering and maturing of the saints, in this life, to the end of the world: and does, by His own presence and Spirit, according to His promise, make them effectual to the saints.[7]

4. This catholic Church has been sometimes more, sometimes less visible.[8] And particular Churches, which are members of it, are more or less pure, to the extent the doctrine of the Gospel is taught and embraced, means of grace administered, and public worship performed more or less purely in them.[9]

5. The purest Churches under heaven are subject both to mixture and error;[10] and some have so degenerated as not to be Churches of Christ,

---

1   Ephesians 1:10,22-23; 5:23,27,32; Colossians 1:18.
2   Psalms 2:8; Romans 15:9-12; 1 Corinthians 1:2; 12:12-13; Revelation 7:9.
3   Genesis 3:15; 17:7; Ezekiel 16:20-21; Acts 2:39; Romans 11:16; 1 Corinthians 7:14.
4   Isaiah 9:7; Matthew 13:47.
5   Ephesians 2:19; 3:15.
6   Acts 2:47.
7   Isaiah 59:21; Matthew 28:19-20; 1 Corinthians 12:28; Ephesians 4:11-13.
8   Romans 11:3-4; Revelation 12:6,14.
9   1 Corinthians 5:6-7; Revelation 2,3.
10 Matthew 13:24-30,47; 1 Corinthians 13:12; Revelation 2,3.

but synagogues of Satan.[1] Nevertheless, there shall be always a Church on earth to worship God according to His will.[2]

6. There is no other head of the Church but the Lord Jesus Christ.[3] Nor can the pope of Rome, in any sense, be head of it.[4]

---

1   Romans 11:18-22; Revelation 18:2.
2   Psalms 72:17; 102:28; Matthew 16:18; 28:19-20.
3   Ephesians 1:22; Colossians 1:18.
4   Matthew 23:8-10; 2 Thessalonians 2:3-4,8-9; Revelation 13:6.

CHAPTER XXVI

OF THE COMMUNION OF SAINTS.

1. All saints, who are united to Jesus Christ their Head, by His Spirit, and by faith, have fellowship with Him in His grace, sufferings, death, resurrection, and glory:[1] and, being united to one another in love, they have communion in each other's gifts and graces,[2] and are obliged to the performance of such duties, public and private, as do contribute to their mutual good, both in the inward and outward man.[3]

2. Those who profess to be saints are bound to maintain a holy fellowship and communion in the worship of God, and in performing such other spiritual services as tend toward their mutual edification;[4] as also in relieving each other in outward things, according to their various abilities and needs. This communion, as God offers opportunity, is to be extended to all those who, in every place, call on the name of the Lord Jesus.[5]

3. This communion that the saints have with Christ, does not make them in any way partakers of the substance of His Godhead; or to be equal with Christ in any respect: to affirm either of these is irreverent and blasphemous.[6] Nor does their communion with each another, as saints, take away, or infringe on the title or ownership that each man has in his goods and possessions.[7]

---

1   John 1:16; Romans 6:5-6; Ephesians 2:5-6; 3:16-19; Philippians 3:10; 2 Timothy 2:12; 1 John 1:3.
2   1 Corinthians 3:21-23; 12:7; Ephesians 4:15-16; Colossians 2:19.
3   Romans 1:11-12,14; Galatians 6:10; 1 Thessalonians 5:11,14; 1 John 3:16-18.
4   Isaiah 2:3; Acts 2:42,46; 1 Corinthians 11:20; Hebrews 10:24-25.
5   Acts 2:44-45; 11:29-30; 2 Corinthians 8,9; 1 John 3:17.
6   Psalms 45:7; Isaiah 42:8; 1 Corinthians 8:6; Colossians 1:18-19; 1 Timothy 6:15-16; Hebrews 1:8-9.
7   Exodus 20:15; Acts 5:4; Ephesians 4:28.

CHAPTER XXVII

OF THE SACRAMENTS.

1. Sacraments are holy signs and seals of the covenant of grace,[1] directly instituted by God,[2] to represent Christ and His benefits; and to confirm our interest in Him:[3] as also, to put a visible difference between those who belong to the Church and the rest of the world;[4] and solemnly to engage them to the service of God in Christ, according to His Word.[5]

2. There is, in every sacrament, a spiritual relationship, or sacramental union, between the sign and the thing signified: so that the names and effects of the one are attributed to the other.[6]

3. The grace that is exhibited in or by the sacraments rightly used, is not conferred by any power in them; neither does the efficacy of a sacrament depend on the piety or intention of him who administers it:[7] but on the work of the Spirit,[8] and the words of institution, which contain, together with a precept authorizing their use, a promise of benefit to those eligible to receive them.[9]

4. There are only two sacraments established by Christ our Lord in the Gospel; that is to say, Baptism, and the Lord's Supper: neither of which may be dispensed by any, but by a minister of the Word lawfully ordained.[10]

5. The sacraments of the Old Testament in regard to the spiritual things thereby signified and exhibited, were, for substance, the same as those of the New.[11]

---

1   Genesis 17:7,10; Romans 4:11.
2   Matthew 28:19; 1 Corinthians 11:23.
3   1 Corinthians 10:16; 11:25-26;
    Galatians 3:17; 3:27.
4   Genesis 34:14; Exodus 12:48; Romans 15:8.
5   Romans 6:3-4; 1 Corinthians 10:16,21.
6   Genesis 17:10; Matthew 26:27-28; Titus 3:5.
7   Romans 2:28-29; 1 Peter 3:21.
8   Matthew 3:11; 1 Corinthians 12:13.
9   Matthew 26:27-28; 28:19-20.
10 Matthew 28:19; 1 Corinthians 4:1; 11:20,23;
    Hebrews 5:4.
11 1 Corinthians 10:1-4.

CHAPTER XXVIII

OF BAPTISM.

1. Baptism is a sacrament of the New Testament, established by Jesus Christ,[1] not only for the solemn admission of the party baptized into the visible Church;[2] but also to be for him a sign and seal of the covenant of grace,[3] of his grafting into Christ,[4] of regeneration,[5] of remission of sins,[6] and of his surrender to God, through Jesus Christ, to walk in newness of life.[7] This sacrament is, by Christ's own appointment, to be continued in His Church until the end of the world.[8]

2. The outward element to be used in this sacrament is water, with which the party is to be baptized, in the name of the Father, and of the Son, and of the Holy Spirit, by a minister of the Gospel, lawfully called to that office.[9]

3. Immersion of the person in the water is not necessary; but Baptism is rightly administered by pouring, or sprinkling water on the person.[10]

4. Not only those who actually profess faith in and obedience to Christ,[11] but also the infants of one, or both, believing parents, are to be baptized.[12]

5. Although it is a great sin to condemn or neglect this ordinance,[13] yet grace and salvation are not so inseparably attached to it, that no person can be regenerated, or saved, without it:[14] or, that all who are baptized are undoubtedly regenerated.[15]

6. The efficacy of Baptism is not tied to that moment of time at which it is administered;[16] yet, notwithstanding, by the right use of this ordinance, the grace promised is not only offered, but really exhibited, and

---

1   Matthew 28:19.
2   1 Corinthians 12:13.
3   Romans 4:11; Colossians 2:11-12.
4   Romans 6:5; Galatians 3:27.
5   Titus 3:5.
6   Mark 1:4.
7   Romans 6:3-4.
8   Matthew 28:19-20.
9   Matthew 3:11; 28:19-20; John 1:33.
10 Mark 7:4; Acts 2:41;16:33; Hebrews 9:10,19-22.

11 Mark 16:15-16; Acts 8:37-38.
12 Genesis 17:7-8; Matthew 28:19; Mark 10:13-16;
    Luke 18:15; Acts 2:38-39; Romans 4:11-12;
    1 Corinthians 7:14; Galatians 3:9,14;
    Colossians 2:11-12.
13 Exodus 4:24-26; Luke 7:30.
14 Acts 10:2,4,22,31,45,47; Romans 4:11.
15 Acts 8:13,23.
16 John 3:5,8.

conferred, by the Holy Spirit, to such (whether of age or infants) as that grace belongs to, according to the counsel of God's own will, in His appointed time.[1]

7. The sacrament of Baptism is but once to be administered to any person.[2]

1   Acts 2:38,41; Galatians 3:27; Ephesians 5:25-26; Titus 3:5.
2   Titus 3:5.

CHAPTER XXIX

OF THE LORD'S SUPPER.

1. Our Lord Jesus, on the night in which He was betrayed, instituted the sacrament of His body and blood, called the Lord's Supper, to be observed in His Church, to the end of the world, for the perpetual remembrance of the sacrifice of Himself in His death; the sealing of all benefits of it to true believers, their spiritual nourishment and growth in Him, their further engagement in and to all duties that they owe to Him; and, to be a bond and pledge of their communion with Him, and with each other, as members of His mystical body.[1]

2. In this sacrament, Christ is not offered up to His Father; nor any real sacrifice made at all, for remission of sins of the living or dead;[2] but only a commemoration of that one offering up of Himself, by Himself, upon the cross, once for all: and a spiritual offering of all possible praise to God, for the same:[3] so that the Roman Catholic sacrifice of the mass (as they call it) is most abominably injurious to Christ's one and only sacrifice, the only propitiation for all the sins of His elect.[4]

3. The Lord Jesus has, in this ordinance, appointed His ministers to declare His words of institution to the people; to pray, and to bless the elements of bread and wine, and thereby to set them apart from a common to a holy use; and to take and break the bread, to take the cup, and (they communicating also themselves) to give both to the communicants;[5] but to none who are not then present in the congregation.[6]

4. Private masses, or receiving this sacrament by a priest, or any other alone;[7] as likewise, the denial of the cup to the people,[8] worshipping the elements, the lifting them up, or carrying them about, for adoration, and the reserving of them for any pretended religious use; are all contrary to the nature of this sacrament, and to the institution of Christ.[9]

1   1 Corinthians 10:16-17,21; 11:23-26; 12:13.
2   Hebrews 9:22,25-26,28.
3   Matthew 26:26-27; 1 Corinthians 11:24-26.
4   Hebrews 7:23-24,27; 10:11-12,14,18.
5   Matthew 26:26-28; Mark 14:22-24;
    Luke 22:19-20; 1 Corinthians 11:23-26.

6   Acts 20:7; 1 Corinthians 11:20.
7   1 Corinthians 10:6.
8   Mark 14:23; 1 Corinthians 11:25-29.
9   Matthew 15:9.

5. The outward elements in this sacrament, duly set apart to the uses ordained by Christ, have such relation to Him crucified, as that, truly, yet sacramentally only, they are sometimes called by the names of the things they represent, to wit, the body and blood of Christ;[1] albeit, in substance and nature, they remain truly and only bread and wine, as they were before.[2]

6. That doctrine that maintains a change of the substance of bread and wine, into the substance of Christ's body and blood (commonly called transubstantiation) by consecration of a priest, or by any other way, is repugnant, not to Scripture alone, but even to common sense, and reason; overthrows the nature of the sacrament; and has been, and is, the cause of many superstitions; even of gross idolatries.[3]

7. Eligible receivers, outwardly partaking of the visible elements, in this sacrament,[4] do then also, inwardly by faith, really and indeed, yet not carnally and corporally but spiritually, receive, and feed on, Christ crucified, and all benefits of His death: the body and blood of Christ being then, not corporally or carnally, in, with, or under the bread and wine; yet, as really, but spiritually, present to the faith of believers in that ordinance, as the elements themselves are to their outward senses.[5]

8. Although ignorant and wicked men receive the outward elements in this sacrament; yet, they receive not the thing signified thereby; but, by their ineligible partaking, are guilty of the body of the Lord, to their own damnation. Wherefore, all ignorant and ungodly persons, as they are unfit to enjoy communion with Him, so are they ineligible for the Lord's table; and cannot, without great sin against Christ, while they remain such, partake of these holy mysteries,[6] or be admitted to them.[7]

---

1 Matthew 26:26-28.
2 Matthew 26:29; 1 Corinthians 11:26-28.
3 Luke 24:6,39; Acts 3:21;
  1 Corinthians 11:24-26.
4 1 Corinthians 11:28.

5 1 Corinthians 10:16.
6 1 Corinthians 11:27-29; 2 Corinthians 6:14,16.
7 Matthew 7:6; 1 Corinthians 5:6-7,13;
  2 Thessalonians 3:6,14-15.

CHAPTER XXX

OF CHURCH CENSURES.

1. The Lord Jesus, as King and Head of His Church, has in it appointed a government, in the hand of Church officers, distinct from the civil magistrate.[1]

2. To these officers the keys of the kingdom of heaven are committed; by virtue of which, they have power, respectively, to retain, and remit sins; to shut that kingdom against the impenitent, both by the Word, and censures; and to open it to penitent sinners, by the ministry of the Gospel; and by absolution from censures, as occasion shall require.[2]

3. Church censures are necessary, for the reclaiming and gaining of offending brothers, for deterring of others from similar offenses, for purging out of that leaven which might infect the whole lump, for vindicating the honor of Christ, and the holy profession of the Gospel, and for preventing the wrath of God, which might justly fall on the Church, if they should suffer His covenant, and the seals thereof, to be profaned by notorious and obstinate offenders.[3]

4. For the better attaining of these ends, the officers of the Church are to proceed by admonition, by suspension from the sacrament of the Lord's Supper for a season; and by excommunication from the Church, according to the nature of the crime, and demerit of the person.[4]

---

1   Isaiah 9:6-7; Matthew 28:18-20; Acts 20:17-18; 1 Corinthians 12:28;
    1 Thessalonians 5:12; 1 Timothy 5:17; Hebrews 13:7,17,24.
2   Matthew 16:19; 18:17-18; John 20:21-23; 2 Corinthians 2:6-8.
3   Matthew 7:6; 1 Corinthians 5,11:27; 1 Timothy 1:20; 5:20; Jude 23.
4   Matthew 18:17; 1 Corinthians 5:4-5,13; 1 Thessalonians 5:12; 2 Thessalonians 3:6,14-15; Titus 3:10.

CHAPTER XXXI

OF SYNODS AND COUNCILS.

1. For the better government, and further edification of the Church, there ought to be such assemblies as are commonly called synods or councils;[1] and it belongs to the overseers and other rulers of the particular churches, by virtue of their office, and the power that Christ has given them for edification and not for destruction, to appoint such assemblies;[2] and to convene together in them, as often as they shall judge it expedient for the good of the Church.[3]

2. It belongs to synods and councils, to determine ministerially controversies of faith, and cases of conscience; to set down rules and directions for the better ordering of the public worship of God, and government of His Church; to receive complaints in cases of improper administration, and to determine authoritatively the same: which decrees and determinations, if consistent with the Word of God, are to be received with reverence and submission; not only for their agreement with the Word, but also for the power by which they are made, as being an ordinance of God appointed in His Word.[4]

3. All synods or councils, since the apostles' times, whether general or particular, may err; and many have erred. Therefore they are not to be made the rule of faith, or practice; but to be used as a help in both.[5]

4. Synods and councils are to handle, or conclude nothing, but that which is ecclesiastical: and are not to meddle in civil affairs that concern the commonwealth, unless by way of humble petition in extraordinary cases; or, by way of advice, for satisfaction of conscience, if they be required to do so by the civil magistrate.[6]

1   Acts 15:2,4,6.
2   Acts 15.
3   Acts 15:22-23,25.
4   Matthew 18:17-20; Acts 15:15,19,24,27-31; 16:4.
5   Acts 17:11; 2 Corinthians 1:24; 2:5; Ephesians 2:20.
6   Luke 12:13-14; John 18:36.

CHAPTER XXXII

OF THE STATE OF MEN AFTER DEATH,
AND OF THE RESURRECTION OF THE DEAD.

1. The bodies of men, after death, return to dust, and see decay:[1] but their souls, which neither die nor sleep, having an immortal existence, immediately return to God who gave them:[2] the souls of the righteous, being then made perfect in holiness, are received into the highest heavens, where they behold the face of God, in light and glory, waiting for the full redemption of their bodies.[3] And the souls of the wicked are cast into hell, where they remain in torments and utter darkness, reserved to the judgment of the great day.[4] Besides these two places, for souls separated from their bodies, the Scripture acknowledges none.

2. At the last day, such as are found alive shall not die, but be changed:[5] and all the dead shall be raised up, with their own bodies, and none other (although with different qualities), which shall be united again to their souls forever.[6]

3. The bodies of the unjust shall, by the power of Christ, be raised to dishonor: the bodies of the just, by His Spirit, to honor; and be made to conform with His own glorious body.[7]

---

1   Genesis 3:19; Acts 13:36.
2   Ecclesiastes 12:7; Luke 23:43.
3   Acts 3:21; 2 Corinthians 5:1,6,8; Ephesians 4:10; Philippians 1:23; Hebrews 12:23.
4   Luke 16:23-24; Acts 1:25; 1 Peter 3:19; Jude 6-7.
5   1 Corinthians 15:51-52; 1 Thessalonians 4:17.
6   Job 19:26-27; 1 Corinthians 15:42-44.
7   John 5:28-29; Acts 24:15; 1 Corinthians 15:43; Philippians 3:21.

CHAPTER XXXIII

OF THE LAST JUDGMENT.

1. God has appointed a day, on which He will judge the world, in righteousness, by Jesus Christ,[1] to whom all power and judgment are given of the Father.[2] In which day, not only the apostate angels shall be judged,[3] but likewise all persons who have lived on earth shall appear before the tribunal of Christ, to give an account of their thoughts, words, and deeds; and to receive according to what they have done in the body, whether good or evil.[4]

2. The purpose of God's appointing this day is to make known the glory of His mercy, in the eternal salvation of the elect; and of His justice, in the damnation of the reprobate, who are wicked and disobedient. For then shall the righteous go to everlasting life, and receive that fullness of joy and refreshing, which shall come from the presence of the Lord: but the wicked, who know not God, and obey not the Gospel of Jesus Christ, shall be cast into eternal torments, and be punished with everlasting destruction from the presence of the Lord, and from the glory of His power.[5]

3. As Christ would have us to be certainly convinced that there shall be a day of judgment, both to deter all men from sin; and for the greater consolation of the godly in their adversity:[6] so will He have that day unknown to men, that they may shake off all worldly security, and be always watchful, because they know not at what hour the Lord will come; and may be ever prepared to say, Come Lord Jesus, come quickly. Amen.[7]

---

1   Acts 17:31.
2   John 5:22,27.
3   1 Corinthians 6:3; 2 Peter 2:4; Jude 6.
4   Ecclesiastes 12:14; Matthew 12:36-37; Romans 2:16; 14:10,12; 2 Corinthians 5:10.
5   Matthew 25:21; 25:31, to the end; Acts 3:19; Romans 2:5-6; 9:22-23; 2 Thessalonians 1:7-10.
6   Luke 27:7,28; Romans 8:23-25; 2 Corinthians 5:10-11; 2 Thessalonians 1:5-7; 2 Peter 3:11,14.
7   Matthew 24:36,42-44; Mark 13:35-37; Luke 12:35-36; Revelation 22:20.

The *Westminster* Larger Catechism

The view of the West Front of Westminster Abbey is one of the best known in the world. The gothic lower part was completed in the fifteenth century; the towers, designed by Nicholas Hawksmoor in a more classical style, were added at the beginning of the eighteenth century.

Anthony Harvey—Sub-Dean of Westminster

Q. 1. What is the chief and highest end of man?

A. Man's chief and highest end is to glorify God,[1] and fully to enjoy Him forever.[2]

Q. 2. How does it appear that there is a God?

A. The very light of nature in man, and the works of God, declare plainly that there is a God;[3] but his Word and Spirit only, do sufficiently and effectually reveal Him to men for their salvation.[4]

Q. 3. What is the Word of God?

A. The holy Scriptures of the Old and New Testaments are the Word of God,[5] the only rule of faith and obedience.[6]

Q. 4. How does it appear that the Scriptures are the Word of God?

A. The Scriptures show themselves to be the Word of God, by their majesty[7] and purity;[8] by the unity of all the parts,[9] and the scope of the whole, which is to give all glory to God;[10] by their light and power to convince and convert sinners, to comfort and build up believers toward salvation.[11] But the Spirit of God, bearing witness by and with the Scriptures in the heart of man, is alone able to convince it fully that they are the very Word of God.[12]

Q. 5. What do the Scriptures principally teach?

A. The Scriptures principally teach, what man is to believe concerning God, and what duty God requires of man.[13]

---

1 Romans 11:36; 1 Corinthians 10:31.
2 Psalm 73:24-28; John 17:21-23.
3 Psalm 19:1-3; Acts 17:28; Romans 1:19-20.
4 Isaiah 59:21; 1 Corinthians 2:9-10; 2 Timothy 3:15-17.
5 2 Timothy 3:16; 2 Peter 1:19-21
6 Isaiah 8:20; Luke 16:29,31; Galatians 1:8-9; Ephesians 2:20; 2 Timothy 3:15-16; Revelation 22:18-19.

7 Psalm 119:18,129; Hosea 8:12; 1 Corinthians 2:6-7,13.
8 Psalm 12:6; 119:140.
9 Acts 10:43; 26:22.
10 Romans 3:19,27.
11 Psalm 19:7-9; Acts 18:28; 20:32; Romans 15:4; James 1:18.
12 John 16:13-14; 20:31; 1 John 2:20,27.
13 2 Timothy 1:13.

WHAT MAN OUGHT TO BELIEVE CONCERNING GOD

Q. 6.   What do the Scriptures make known of God?

A.   The Scriptures make known what God is,[1] the persons in the Godhead,[2] his decrees,[3] and the execution of his decrees.[4]

Q. 7.   What is God?

A.   God is a Spirit,[5] in and of Himself infinite in being,[6] glory,[7] blessedness,[8] and perfection;[9] all-sufficient,[10] eternal,[11] unchangeable,[12] incomprehensible,[13] everywhere present,[14] almighty;[15] knowing all things,[16] most wise,[17] most holy,[18] most just,[19] most merciful and gracious, long-suffering, and abundant in goodness and truth.[20]

Q. 8.   Are there more Gods than one?

A.   There is but one only, the living and true God.[21]

Q. 9.   How many persons are there in the Godhead?

A.   There are three persons in the Godhead: the Father, the Son, and the Holy Spirit; and these three are one true, eternal God, the same in substance, equal in power and glory; although distinguished by their personal properties.[22]

Q. 10.   What are the personal properties of the three persons in the Godhead?

A.   It is the property of the Father to beget His Son,[23] and of the Son to be begotten of the Father,[24] and of the Holy Spirit to proceed from the Father and the Son, from all eternity.[25]

1   Hebrews 11:6.
2   1 John 5:17.
3   Acts 15:14-15,18.
4   Acts 4:27-28.
5   John 4:24.
6   Exodus 3:14; Job 11:7-9.
7   Acts 7:2.
8   1 Timothy 6:15.
9   Matthew 5:48.
10   Genesis 17:1.
11   Psalm 90:2.
12   Malachi 3:6.
13   1 Kings 8:27.
14   Psalm 139:1-13.
15   Revelation 4:8.
16   Psalm 147:5; Hebrews 4:13.
17   Romans 16:27.
18   Isaiah 8:3.
19   Deuteronomy 32:4.
20   Exodus 34:6.
21   Deuteronomy 6:4; Jeremiah 10:10; 1 Corinthians 8:4,6.
22   Matthew 3:16-17; 28:19; John 10:30; 2 Corinthians 13:14; 1 John 5:7.
23   Hebrews 1:5-6,8.
24   John 1:14,18.
25   John 15:26; Galatians 4:6.

Q. 11.   How does it appear that the Son and the Holy Spirit are equal with the Father?

A.   The Scriptures show that the Son and the Holy Spirit are God equal with the Father, ascribing to them such names,[1] attributes,[2] works,[3] and worship,[4] as are proper to God only.

Q. 12.   What are the decrees of God?

A.   God's decrees are the wise, free, and holy acts of the counsel of His will,[45] whereby, from all eternity, He has, for his own glory, unchangeably foreordained whatever comes to pass in time,[6] especially concerning angels and men.

Q. 13.   What has God especially decreed concerning angels and men?

A.   God, by an eternal and unchangeable decree, out of His mere love, for the praise of His glorious grace, to be made known at the appropriate time, has elected some angels to glory;[7] and, in Christ, has chosen some men to eternal life, and the means for this;[8] and also, according to His sovereign power, and the unsearchable counsel of His own will (with which he extends or withholds favor as he pleases), has passed by, and foreordained the rest to dishonor and wrath, to be inflicted because of their sin, to the praise of the glory of His justice.[9]

Q. 14.   How does God execute his decrees?

A.   God executes His decrees in the works of creation and providence, according to His infallible foreknowledge, and the free and unchangeable counsel of His own will.[10]

Q. 15.   What is the work of creation?

A.   The work of creation is that in which God did in the beginning, by the word of his power, make of nothing, the world and all

1   Isaiah 6:3,5,8; John 12:41; Acts 5:3-4; 28:25; 1 John 5:20.
2   Isaiah 9:5; John 1:1; 2:24-25; 1 Corinthians 2:10-11.
3   Genesis 1:2; Colossians 1:16.
4   Matthew 28:19; 2 Corinthians 8:14.
5   Romans 9:14-15,18; 11:33; Ephesians 1:11.
6   Psalm 33:11; Romans 9:22-23; Ephesians 1:4,11.
7   1 Timothy 5:21.
8   Ephesians 1:4-6; 2 Thessalonians 2:13-14.
9   Matthew 11:25-26; Romans 9:17-18,21-22; 2 Timothy 2:20; 1 Peter 2:8; Jude 4.
10   Ephesians 1:11.

things therein, for Himself, within the space of six days, and all very good.[1]

Q. 16. How did God create angels?

A. God created all the angels[2] as spirits,[3] immortal,[4] holy, excelling in knowledge,[5] mighty in power;[6] to execute His commandments, and to praise His name,[7] yet subject to change.[8]

Q. 17. How did God create man?

A. After God had made all other creatures, He created man, male and female;[9] formed the body of the man of the dust of the ground,[10] and the woman of the rib of man,[11] endued them with living, reasonable, and immortal souls;[12] made them after His own image,[13] in knowledge,[14] righteousness, and holiness,[15] having the law of God written in their hearts,[16] and power to fulfill it,[17] with dominion over the creatures;[18] yet subject to fall.[19]

Q. 18. What are God's works of providence?

A. God's works of providence are His most holy,[20] wise,[21] and powerful preserving[22] and governing[23] all his creatures; using them, and all their actions,[24] to His own glory.[25]

Q. 19. What is God's providence toward the angels?

A. God by his providence permitted some of the angels, willfully and irreversibly, to fall into sin and damnation,[26] limiting and

---

1   Genesis 1; Proverbs 16:4; Hebrews 11:3.
2   Colossians 1:16.
3   Psalm 104:4.
4   Matthew 22:30.
5   2 Samuel 14:17; Matthew 24:36.
6   2 Thessalonians 1:7.
7   Psalm 103:20-21.
8   2 Peter 2:4.
9   Genesis 1:27.
10 Genesis 2:7.
11 Genesis 2:22.
12 Genesis 2:7; Job 35:11; Ecclesiastes 12:7; Matthew 10:28; Luke 23:43.
13 Genesis 1:27.
14 Colossians 3:10.
15 Ephesians 4:24.
16 Romans 2:14-15.
17 Ecclesiastes 7:29.
18 Genesis 1:28.
19 Genesis 3:6; Ecclesiastes 7:29.
20 Psalm 145:17.
21 Psalm 104:24.
22 Hebrews 1:3.
23 Psalm 103:19.
24 Genesis 45:7; Matthew 10:29-31.
25 Isaiah 63:14; Romans 11:36.
26 John 8:4; Hebrews 2:16; 2 Peter 2:4; Jude 6.

using that, and all their sins, to His own glory;[1] and established the rest in holiness and happiness;[2] employing them all,[3] at His pleasure, in the administration of His power, mercy, and justice.[4]

Q. 20.   What was the providence of God toward man in the estate in which he was created?

A.   The providence of God toward man in the estate in which he was created was, the placing of him in paradise, appointing him to take care of it, giving him liberty to eat of the fruit of the earth,[5] putting the creatures under his dominion,[6] ordaining marriage for his help,[7] affording him communion with Himself,[8] and instituting the Sabbath;[9] entering into a covenant of life with him, upon condition of personal, perfect, and perpetual obedience,[10] of which the Tree of Life was a pledge;[11] and forbidding him to eat of the Tree of the Knowledge of Good and Evil, on pain of death.[12]

Q. 21.   Did man continue in that estate in which God created him?

A.   Our first parents, being left to the freedom of their own will, through the temptation of Satan, transgressed the commandment of God, in eating the forbidden fruit, and thereby fell from the estate of innocence in which they were created.[13]

Q. 22.   Did all mankind fall in that first transgression?

A.   The covenant being made with Adam as a representative person, not for himself only, but for his descendants, all mankind, descending from him by ordinary generation,[14] sinned in him, and fell with him in that first transgression.[15]

1   Job 1:12; Matthew 8:31.
2   Mark 8:38; 1 Timothy 5:21; Hebrews 12:22.
3   Psalm 104:4.
4   2 Kings 19:35; Hebrews 1:14.
5   Genesis 2:8,15-16.
6   Genesis 1:28.
7   Genesis 2:18.
8   Genesis 1:26-29; 3:8.
9   Genesis 2:3.
10   Romans 10:5; Galatians 3:1.
11   Genesis 2:9.
12   Genesis 2:17.
13   Genesis 3:6-8,13; Ecclesiastes 7:29;
     2 Corinthians 11:3.
14   Acts 17:26.
15   Genesis 2:16-17; Romans 5:12-20; 1
     Corinthians 15: 21-22.

Q. 23.   Into what estate did the Fall bring mankind?

A.   The Fall brought mankind into an estate of sin
         and misery.[1]

Q. 24.   What is sin?

A.   Sin is any lack of conformity to, or transgression of, any law of
         God, given as a rule to the reasonable creature.[2]

Q. 25.   What is the sinfulness of that estate into which man fell?

A.   The sinfulness of that estate into which man fell, consists of the
         guilt of Adam's first sin,[3] the lack of that righteousness in which
         he was created, and the corruption of his nature, through which
         he is made utterly unwilling, unable, and opposite to all that is
         spiritually good, and wholly inclined to all evil, and that contin-
         ually;[4] which is commonly called original sin, and from which
         do proceed all actual transgressions.[5]

Q. 26.   How is original sin conveyed from our first parents to their
         descendants?

A.   Original sin is conveyed from our first parents to their descen-
         dants by natural generation, so as all that proceed from them in
         that way, are conceived and born in sin.[6]

Q. 27.   What misery did the Fall bring on mankind?

A.   The Fall brought on mankind the loss of communion with
         God,[7] His displeasure and curse; so as we are by nature chil-
         dren of wrath,[8] bond slaves to Satan,[9] and justly liable to all
         punishments in this world and that which is to come.[10]

Q. 28.   What are the punishments of sin in this world?

A.   The punishments of sin in this world, are either inward, as blind-
         ness of mind,[11] a reprobate sense,[12] strong delusions,[13] hard-
         ness of heart,[14] horror of conscience,[15] and vile affections;[16] or

1   Romans 3:23; 5:12.
2   Galatians 3:10,12; 1 John 3:4.
3   Romans 5:12,19.
4   Genesis 6:5; Romans 3:10-19; 5:6; 8:7-8;
     Ephesians 2:1-3.
5   Matthew 15:19; James 1:14-15.
6   Job 14:4; 15:14; Psalm 51:5; John 3:6.
7   Genesis 3:8,10,24.
8   Ephesians 2:2-3.

9   2 Timothy 2:26.
10   Genesis 2:17; Lamentations 3:39;
     Matthew 25:41,46; Romans 6:23; Jude 7.
11   Ephesians 4:18.
12   Romans 1:28.
13   2 Thessalonians 2:11.
14   Romans 2:5.
15   Genesis 4:13; Isaiah 33:14; Matthew 27:4.
16   Romans 1:26.

outward, as the curse of God on the creatures for our sake,[1] and all other evils that befall us in our bodies, names, estates, relations, and employments;[2] together with death itself.[3]

Q. 29. What are the punishments of sin in the world to come?

A. The punishments of sin in the world to come are everlasting separation from the comforting presence of God, and most grievous torments in soul and body, without relief, in hellfire forever.[4]

Q. 30. Does God leave all mankind to perish in the estate of sin and misery?

A. God does not leave all men to perish in the estate of sin and misery,[5] into which they fell by the breach of the first covenant, commonly called the Covenant of Works;[6] but of his mere love and mercy delivers His elect out of it, and brings them into an estate of salvation by the second covenant, commonly called the Covenant of Grace.[7]

Q. 31. With whom was the Covenant of Grace made?

A. The Covenant of Grace was made with Christ as the second Adam, and in Him with all the elect as His seed.[8]

Q. 32. How is the grace of God shown in the second covenant?

A. The grace of God is shown in the second covenant, in that He freely provides and offers to sinners a Mediator,[9] and life and salvation by Him;[10] and requiring faith as the condition to interest them in Him,[11] promises and gives His Holy Spirit[12] to all His elect, to work in them that faith,[13] with all other saving graces;[14] and to enable them to do all holy obedience,[15] as the evidence of the truth of their faith[16] and of their thankfulness to

---

1 Genesis 3:17.
2 Deuteronomy 28:15-18.
3 Romans 6:21,23.
4 Mark 9:43-44,46,48; Luke 16:24;
   2 Thessalonians 1:9.
5 1 Thessalonians 5:9.
6 Galatians 3:10,12.
7 Romans 3:20; 2 Corinthians 3:7-9;
   Galatians 3:21; Titus 3:4-7.

8 Isaiah 53:10-11; Romans 5:15-21;
   Galatians 3:16.
9 Genesis 3:15; Isaiah 42:6; John 6:27.
10 1 John 5:11-12.
11 John 1:12; 3:16.
12 Proverbs 1:23.
13 2 Corinthians 4:13.
14 Galatians 5:22-23.
15 Ezekiel 36:27.
16 James 2:18,22.

God,[1] and as the way which he has appointed them to salvation.[2]

Q. 33.   Was the Covenant of Grace always administered in one and the same manner?

A.   The Covenant of Grace was not always administered in the same manner, but the administrations of it under the Old Testament were different from those under the New.[3]

Q. 34.   How was the Covenant of Grace administered under the Old Testament?

A.   The Covenant of Grace was administered under the Old Testament, by promises,[4] prophecies,[5] sacrifices,[6] circumcision,[7] the Passover,[8] and other types and ordinances; which did all signify Christ then to come, and were for that time sufficient to build up the elect in faith in the promised Messiah,[9] by whom they then had full remission of sin and eternal salvation.[10]

Q. 35.   How is the Covenant of Grace administered under the New Testament?

A.   Under the New Testament, when Christ appeared in the flesh, the same Covenant of Grace was, and still is to be, administered in the preaching of the Word,[11] and the administration of the sacraments of Baptism,[12] and the Lord's Supper;[13] in which grace and salvation are shown in more fullness, evidence, and efficacy to all nations.[14]

Q. 36.   Who is the Mediator of the Covenant of Grace?

A.   The only Mediator of the Covenant of Grace is the Lord Jesus Christ,[15] who being the eternal Son of God, of one substance and equal with the Father,[16] in the fullness of time became

1   2 Corinthians 5:14-15.
2   Ephesians 2:18.
3   2 Corinthians 3:6-7,21-22.
4   Romans 15:8.
5   Acts 3:20,24.
6   Hebrews 10:1.
7   Romans 4:11.
8   1 Corinthians 5:7.
9   Hebrews 8; 9; 10; 11; 13.
10   Galatians 3:7-9,14.
11   Mark 16:15.
12   Matthew 28:19-20.
13   1 Corinthians 11:23-25.
14   Matthew 28:19; 2 Corinthians 3:6-9;
     Hebrews 8:6,10-11.
15   1 Timothy 2:5.
16   John 1:1,14; 10:30; Philippians 2:6.

man,[1] and so was, and continues to be, God and man, in two entire distinct natures, and one person, forever.[2]

Q. 37. How did Christ, being the Son of God, become man?

A. Christ, the Son of God, became man by taking to Himself a true body, and a reasonable soul,[3] being conceived by the power of the Holy Spirit, in the womb of the Virgin Mary, of her substance, and born of her,[4] yet without sin.[5]

Q. 38. Why was it necessary that the Mediator should be God?

A. It was necessary that the Mediator should be God; that he might sustain and keep the human nature from sinking under the infinite wrath of God, and the power of death;[6] give worth and efficacy to His sufferings, obedience, and intercession;[7] and to satisfy God's justice,[8] procure His favor, purchase a unique people,[9] give His Spirit to them,[10] conquer all their enemies,[11] and bring them to everlasting salvation.[12]

Q. 39. Why was it necessary that the Mediator should be man?

A. It was necessary that the Mediator should be man; that he might advance our nature,[13] perform obedience to the law,[14] suffer and make intercession for us in our nature,[15] have a fellow feeling of our infirmities;[16] that we might receive the adoption of sons,[17] and have comfort and access with boldness to the Throne of Grace.[18]

Q. 40. Why was it necessary that the Mediator should be God and man in one person?

A. It was necessary that the Mediator, who was to reconcile God and man, should Himself be both God and man, and this in one person; that the proper works of each nature might be accepted of God for us,[19] and relied on by us, as the works of the whole person.[20]

---

1 Galatians 4:4.
2 Luke 1:35; Romans 9:5; Colossians 2:9; Hebrews 7:24-25.
3 Matthew 26:38; John 1:14.
4 Luke 1:27,31,35,42; Galatians 4:4.
5 Hebrews 4:15; 7:26.
6 Acts 2:24-25; Romans 1:4; 4:25; Hebrews 9:14.
7 Acts 20:28; Hebrews 7:25-28; 9:14.
8 Romans 3:24-26.
9 Titus 2:13-14.
10 Galatians 4:6.
11 Luke 1:68-69,71,74.
12 Hebrews 5:8-9; 9:11-15.
13 Hebrews 2:16.
14 Galatians 4:4.
15 Hebrews 2:14; 7:24-25.
16 Hebrews 4:15.
17 Galatians 4:5.
18 Hebrews 4:16.
19 Matthew 1:21,23; 3:17; Hebrews 9:14.
20 1 Peter 2:6.

Q. 41.   Why was our Mediator called Jesus?

A.   Our Mediator was called Jesus, because he saves His people from their sins.[1]

Q. 42.   Why was our Mediator called Christ?

A.   Our Mediator was called Christ, because he was anointed with the Holy Spirit above measure;[2] and so set apart, and fully furnished with all authority and ability,[3] to execute the office of prophet,[4] priest,[5] and king of His church,[6] in the estate both of His humiliation and exaltation.

Q. 43.   How does Christ execute the office of a prophet?

A.   Christ executes the office of a prophet, in his revealing to the church[7] in all ages, by his Spirit and Word,[8] in various ways of administration,[9] the whole will of God,[10] in all things concerning their edification and salvation.[11]

Q. 44.   How does Christ execute the office of a priest?

A.   Christ executes the office of a priest, in His once offering Himself as a sacrifice without imperfection to God,[12] to be a reconciliation for the sins of His people;[13] and in making continual intercession for them.[14]

Q. 45.   How does Christ execute the office of a king?

A.   Christ executes the office of a king, in calling out of the world a people to Himself;[15] and giving them officers,[16] laws,[17] and censures, by which he visibly governs them;[18] in bestowing saving grace on His elect,[19] rewarding their obedience,[20] and correcting them for their sins,[21] preserving and supporting them

---

1   Matthew 1:21.
2   Psalm 45:7; John 3:34.
3   Matthew 28:18-20; John 6:7.
4   Luke 4:18,21; Acts 3:21-22.
5   Hebrews 4:14-15; 5:5-7.
6   Psalm 2:6; Isaiah 9:6-7; Matthew 21:5; Philippians 2:8-11.
7   John 1:18.
8   1 Peter 1:10-12.
9   Hebrews 1:1-2.
10   John 15:15.
11   John 20:31; Acts 20:23; Ephesians 4:11-13.

12   Hebrews 9:14,28.
13   Hebrews 2:17.
14   Hebrews 7:25.
15   Genesis 49:10; Psalm 110:3; Isaiah 55:4-5; Acts 15:14-16.
16   1 Corinthians 12:28; Ephesians 4:11-12.
17   Isaiah 33:22.
18   Matthew 18:17-18; 1 Corinthians 5:4-5.
19   Acts 5:31.
20   Revelation 2:10; 22:12.
21   Revelation 3:19.

under all their temptations and sufferings;[1] restraining and overcoming all their enemies,[2] and powerfully ordering all things for
His own glory,[3] and their good;[4] and also in taking vengeance
on the rest, who know not God, and obey not the Gospel.[5]

Q. 46.   What was the estate of Christ's humiliation?

A.   The estate of Christ's humiliation was that low condition,
           wherein He, for our sakes, emptying himself of His glory, took
           upon Himself the form of a servant, in His conception and
           birth, life, death, and after His death until His resurrection.[6]

Q. 47.   How did Christ humble Himself in his conception and birth?

A.   Christ humbled Himself in His conception and birth, in that,
           being from all eternity the Son of God in the bosom of the
           Father, he was pleased in the fullness of time to become the
           Son of Man, made of a woman of low estate, and to be born to
           her, with various circumstances of more than ordinary depriva-
           tion.[7]

Q. 48.   How did Christ humble Himself in His life?

A.   Christ humbled Himself in His life, by subjecting Himself to the
           law,[8] which He perfectly fulfilled,[9] and by enduring the indig-
           nities of the world,[10] temptations of Satan,[11] and infirmities in
           His flesh; whether common to the nature of man, or particularly
           accompanying His low condition.[12]

Q. 49.   How did Christ humble Himself in His death?

A.   Christ humbled Himself in His death in that, having been
           betrayed by Judas,[13] forsaken by His disciples,[14] scorned and
           rejected by the world,[15] condemned by Pilate, and tormented
           by His persecutors;[16] having also conflicted with the terrors of
           death and the powers of darkness, having felt and borne the

---

1   Isaiah 63:9.
2   Psalm 110:1-2; 1 Corinthians 15:25.
3   Romans 14:10-11.
4   Romans 8:28.
5   Psalm 2:8-9; 2 Thessalonians 1:8-9.
6   Luke 1:31; Acts 2:24; 2 Corinthians 8:8;
    Philippians 2:6-8.
7   Luke 2:7; John 1:14,18; Galatians 4:4.
8   Galatians 4:4.

9   Matthew 5:17; Romans 5:19.
10 Psalm 22:6; Hebrews 12:2-3.
11 Matthew 4:1-12; Luke 4:13.
12 Isaiah 52:13-14; Hebrews 2:17-18; 4:15.
13 Matthew 27:4.
14 Matthew 26:56.
15 Isaiah 53:2-3.
16 Matthew 27:26-50; John 29:34.

weight of God's wrath,[1] He laid down his life an offering for sin,[2] enduring the painful, shameful, and cursed death of the cross.[3]

Q. 50. In what did Christ's humiliation consist after His death?

A. Christ's humiliation after His death consisted in His being buried,[4] and continuing in the state of the dead, and under the power of death till the third day,[5] which has been otherwise expressed in these words: "He descended into hell."

Q. 51. What was the estate of Christ's exaltation?

A. The estate of Christ's exaltation is made up of His resurrection,[6] ascension,[7] sitting at the right hand of the Father,[8] and His coming again to judge the world.[9]

Q. 52. How was Christ exalted in His resurrection?

A. Christ was exalted in His resurrection, in that, not having seen decay in death (in which it was not possible for Him to be held),[10] and having the very same body in which he suffered, with its essential properties[11] (but without mortality and other common infirmities belonging to this life), really united to His soul,[12] He rose again from the dead the third day by His own power;[13] whereby He declared Himself to be the Son of God,[14] to have satisfied divine justice,[15] to have vanquished death and him who had the power of it,[16] and to be Lord of the living and the dead.[17] All this He did as a representative person,[18] the head of His church,[19] for their justification,[20] making them alive in grace,[21] supporting them against enemies,[22] and assuring them of their resurrection from the dead at the last day.[23]

1 Matthew 27:46; Luke 22:44.
2 Isaiah 53:10.
3 Galatians 3:13; Philippians 2:8; Hebrews 12:2.
4 1 Corinthians 15:3-4.
5 Psalm 16:10; Matthew 12:40; Acts 2:24-27,31; Romans 6:9.
6 1 Corinthians 15:4.
7 Mark 16:19.
8 Ephesians 1:20.
9 Acts 1:11; 17:31.
10 Acts 2:24,27.
11 Luke 24:39.
12 Romans 6:9; Revelation 1:18.
13 John 10:17-18.
14 Romans 1:4.
15 Romans 8:34.
16 Hebrews 2:14.
17 Romans 14:9.
18 1 Corinthians 15:21-22.
19 Ephesians 1:20-23; Colossians 1:18.
20 Romans 4:25.
21 Ephesians 2:1,5-6; Colossians 2:12.
22 1 Corinthians 15:25-27.
23 1 Corinthians 15:20.

Q. 53.   How was Christ exalted in his ascension?

A.   Christ was exalted in His ascension, in that having, after His resurrection, often appeared to and conversed with His apostles, speaking to them of the things pertaining to the Kingdom of God,[1] and giving them commission to preach the gospel to all nations;[2] forty days after His resurrection, He, in our nature, and as our Head,[3] triumphing over enemies,[4] visibly went up into the highest heavens, there to receive gifts for men,[5] to raise up our affections in that way,[6] and to prepare a place for us,[7] where He is, and shall continue till His second coming at the end of the world.[8]

Q. 54.   How is Christ exalted in His sitting at the right hand of God?

A.   Christ is exalted in His sitting at the right hand of God, in that as God-man He is advanced to the highest favor with God the Father,[9] with all fullness of joy,[10] glory,[11] and power over all things in heaven and earth;[12] and does gather and defend His church, and subdue their enemies; furnishes His ministers and people with gifts and graces,[13] and makes intercession for them.[14]

Q. 55.   How does Christ make intercession?

A.   Christ makes intercession, by His appearing in our nature continually before the Father in heaven,[15] in the merit of His obedience and sacrifice on earth;[16] declaring His will to have it applied to all believers;[17] answering all accusations against them;[18] and obtaining for them peace of conscience, notwithstanding daily failings,[19] access with boldness to the Throne of Grace,[20] and acceptance of them[21] and their services.[22]

1   Acts 1:2-3.
2   Matthew 28:19-20.
3   Hebrews 6:20.
4   Ephesians 4:8.
5   Psalm 66:18; Acts 1:9-11; Ephesians 4:10.
6   Colossians 3:1-2.
7   John 14:3.
8   Acts 3:21.
9   Philippians 2:9.
10 Psalm 16:11; Acts 2:28.
11 John 17:5.
12 Ephesians 1:22; 1 Peter 3:22.
13 Psalm 110:1; Ephesians 4:10-12.
14 Romans 8:34.
15 Hebrews 9:12,24.
16 Hebrews 1:3.
17 John 3:16; 17:9,20,24.
18 Romans 8:33-34.
19 Romans 5:1-2; 1 John 2:1-2.
20 Hebrews 4:16.
21 Ephesians 1:6.
22 1 Peter 2:5.

Q. 56. How is Christ to be exalted in His coming again to judge the world?

A. Christ is to be exalted in his coming again to judge the world, in that He, who was unjustly judged and condemned by wicked men,[1] shall come again at the last day in great power,[2] and in the full display of His own glory, and of His Father's, with all his holy angels,[3] with a shout, with the voice of the archangel, and with the trumpet of God,[4] to judge the world in righteousness.[5]

Q. 57. What benefits has Christ obtained by his mediation?

A. Christ by His mediation has obtained redemption,[6] with all other benefits of the Covenant of Grace.[7]

Q. 58. How do we come to be made recipients of the benefits that Christ has obtained?

A. We are made recipients of the benefits that Christ has obtained, by the application of them to us,[8] which is the work especially of God the Holy Spirit.[9]

Q. 59. Who are made recipients of redemption through Christ?

A. Redemption is certainly applied, and effectually communicated, to all those for whom Christ has purchased it;[10] who are at the appropriate time enabled by the Holy Spirit to believe in Christ, according to the Gospel.[11]

Q. 60. Can they who have never heard the Gospel, and thus do not know Jesus Christ or believe in Him, be saved by their living according to the light of nature?

A. They who, having never heard the Gospel,[12] do not know Jesus Christ[13] and do not believe in Him, cannot be saved,[14] though they be diligent to frame their lives according to the light of

1   Acts 3:14-15.
2   Matthew 24:30.
3   Matthew 25:31; Luke 9:26.
4   1 Thessalonians 4:16.
5   Acts 17:31.
6   Hebrews 9:12,
7   2 Corinthians 1:20.
8   John 1:11-12.
9   Titus 3:5-6.
10 John 6:37,39; 10:15-16; Ephesians 1:13-14.
11 2 Corinthians 4:13; Ephesians 2:8.
12 Romans 10:14.
13 John 1:10-12; Ephesians 2:12; 2 Thessalonians 1:8-9.
14 Mark 16:16; John 8:24.

nature,[1] or the laws of that religion which they profess;[2] neither is there salvation in any other, but in Christ alone,[3] who is the Savior only of His body the church.[4]

Q. 61. Are all saved who hear the Gospel, and live in the church?

A. All who hear the Gospel, and live in the visible church, are not saved; but only they who are true members of the church invisible.[5]

Q. 62. What is the visible church?

A. The visible church is a society made up of all persons who in all ages and places of the world do profess the true religion,[6] and of their children.[7]

Q. 63. What are the special privileges of the visible church?

A. The visible church has the privilege of being under God's special care and government;[8] of being protected and preserved in all ages, notwithstanding the opposition of all enemies;[9] and of enjoying the communion of saints, the ordinary means of salvation,[10] and offers of grace by Christ, to all members of it, in the ministry of the Gospel, testifying that whoever believes in Him shall be saved,[11] and excluding none who will come to Him.[12]

Q. 64. What is the invisible church?

A. The invisible church is the whole number of the elect, who have been, are, or shall be gathered into one under Christ the head.[13]

1 1 Corinthians 1:20-24.
2 John 4:22; Romans 9:31-32; Philippians 3:4-9.
3 Acts 4:12.
4 Ephesians 5:23.
5 Matthew 7:21; 22:14; John 12:38-40; Romans 9:6; 11:7.
6 Psalm 2:8; 22:27-31; 45:17; Isaiah 59:21; Matthew 28:19-20; Romans 15:9-12; 1 Corinthians 1:2; 12-13; Revelation 7:9.
7 Genesis 17:7; Acts 2:39; Romans 11:16; 1 Corinthians 7:14.
8 Isaiah 9:5-6; 1 Timothy 4:10.
9 Psalm 115:1-2,9; Isaiah 31:4-5; Zechariah 12:2-4,8,9.
10 Acts 2:39,42.
11 Psalm 147:19-20; Mark 16:15-16; Romans 9:4; Ephesians 4:11-12.
12 John 6:37.
13 John 10:16; 11:52; Ephesians 1:10,22-23.

Q. 65. What special benefits do the members of the invisible church enjoy by Christ?

A. The members of the invisible church, by Christ, enjoy union and communion with Him in grace and glory.[1]

Q. 66. What is that union that the elect have with Christ?

A. The union that the elect have with Christ is the work of God's grace,[2] by which they are spiritually and mystically, yet really and inseparably, joined to Christ as their head and husband;[3] which is done in their effectual calling[4]

Q. 67. What is effectual calling?

A. Effectual calling is the work of God's almighty power and grace,[5] by which (out of his free and special love to his elect, and from nothing in them moving him to do so)[6] He does in his accepted time invite and draw them to Jesus Christ, by His Word and Spirit;[7] savingly enlightening their minds,[8] renewing and powerfully determining their wills,[9] so as they (although in themselves dead in sin) are hereby made willing and able, freely to answer His call, and to accept and embrace the grace offered and conveyed in it.[10]

Q. 68. Are the elect only effectually called?

A. All the elect, and they only, are effectually called;[11] although others may be, and often are, outwardly called by the ministry of the Word,[12] and have some common operations of the Spirit,[13] who, for their willful neglect and contempt of the grace offered to them, being justly left in their unbelief, do never truly come to Jesus Christ.[14]

1 John 17:21,24; Ephesians 2:5-6.
2 Ephesians 1:22; 2:6-7.
3 John 10:28; 1 Corinthians 6:17; Ephesians 5:23,30.
4 1 Corinthians 1:9; 1 Peter 5:10.
5 John 5:25; Ephesians 1:18-20; 2 Timothy 1:8-9.
6 Romans 9:11; Ephesians 2:4-5,7-9; Titus 3:4-5.
7 John 6:44; 2 Corinthians 5:20; 6:1-2; 2 Thessalonians 2:13-14.
8 Acts 26:18; 1 Corinthians 2:10,12.
9 Ezekiel 11:19; 36:26-27; John 6:45.
10 Deuteronomy 30:6; Ephesians 2:5; Philippians 2:13.
11 Acts 13:48.
12 Matthew 22:14.
13 Matthew 7:22; 13:20-21; Hebrews 6:4-6.
14 Psalm 81:11-12; John 6:64-65; 12:38-40; Acts 28:25-27.

Q. 69.   What is the communion in grace, which the members of the invisible church have with Christ?

A.   The communion in grace, which the members of the invisible church have with Christ, is their partaking of the virtue of His mediation, in their justification,[1] adoption,[2] sanctification, and whatever else in this life demonstrates their union with Him.[3]

Q. 70.   What is justification?

A.   Justification is an act of God's free grace to sinners,[4] in which He pardons all their sin, accepts and accounts them righteous in His sight;[5] not for anything done in them, or done by them,[6] but only for the perfect obedience and full satisfaction of Christ, imputed to them by God[7] and received by faith alone.[8]

Q. 71.   How is justification an act of God's free grace?

A.   Although Christ, by his obedience and death, did make a proper, real, and full satisfaction of God's justice on behalf of them who are justified:[9] yet inasmuch as God accepts the satisfaction from a surety, which he might have demanded of them; and did provide this surety, His only Son,[10] imputing his righteousness to them,[11] and requiring nothing of them for their justification, but faith,[12] which also is His gift,[13] their justification is to them of free grace.[14]

Q. 72.   What is justifying faith?

A.   Justifying faith is a saving grace,[15] wrought in the heart of a sinner, by the Spirit[16] and the Word of God;[17] whereby he, being convinced of his sin and misery, and of his own inability and the inability of all other creatures to rescue him from his lost condition,[18] not only assents to the truth of the promise of the Gospel,[19] but receives and rests on Christ and His righteousness

1   Romans 8:30.
2   Ephesians 1:5.
3   1 Corinthians 1:30.
4   Romans 3:22,24-25; 4:5.
5   Romans 3:22,24-25,27-28; 2 Corinthians 5:19-21.
6   Ephesians 1:7; Titus 3:5,7.
7   Romans 4:6-8; 5:17-19.
8   Acts 10:43; Galatians 2:16; Philippians 3:9.
9   Romans 5:8-10,19.
10   Isaiah 53:4-6,10-12; Daniel 9:24,26;
Matthew 20:28; Romans 8:32; 1 Timothy 2:5-6;
Hebrews 7:22; 10:10; 1 Peter 1:18-19.
11   2 Corinthians 5:21.
12   Romans 3:24-25.
13   Ephesians 2:8.
14   Ephesians 1:17.
15   Hebrews 10:39.
16   2 Corinthians 4:13; Ephesians 1:17-19.
17   Romans 10:14-17.
18   John 16:8-9; Acts 2:37; 4:12; 16:30;
Romans 6:8; Ephesians 2:1.
19   Ephesians 1:13.

held forth in that truth, for pardon of sin,[1] and for the accepting and accounting of him as righteous in the sight of God for salvation.[2]

Q. 73.   How does faith justify a sinner in the sight of God?

A.   Faith justifies a sinner in the sight of God, not because of those other graces that always accompany it, or because of good works that are the fruits of it;[3] nor as if the grace of faith, or any act of it, were imputed to him for justification;[4] but only as it is an instrument, by which he receives and applies Christ and His righteousness.[5]

Q. 74.   What is adoption?

A.   Adoption is an act of the free grace of God,[6] in and for His only Son Jesus Christ,[7] by which all those who are justified are received into the number of His children,[8] have His name put on them,[9] the Spirit of His Son given to them,[10] are under His Fatherly care and dispensations,[11] admitted to all the liberties and privileges of the sons of God, made heirs of all the promises, and fellow heirs with Christ in glory.[12]

Q. 75.   What is sanctification?

A.   Sanctification is a work of God's grace, by which they, whom God has, before the foundation of the world, chosen to be holy, are, in time, through the powerful operation of His Spirit,[13] applying the death and resurrection of Christ to them,[14] renewed in their whole man after the image of God;[15] having the seeds of repentance to life, and all other saving graces, put into their hearts,[16] and those graces so stirred up, increased and strengthened,[17] as that they more and more die to sin, and rise to newness of life.[18]

---

1   John 1:12; Acts 10:43; 16:31.

2   Acts 15:11; Philippians 3:9.

3   Romans 3:28; Galatians 3:11.

4   Romans 4:5; 10:10.

5   John 1:12; Galatians 1:16; Philippians 3:9.

6   1 John 3:1.

7   Galatians 4:4-5; Ephesians 1:5.

8   John 1:12.

9   2 Corinthians 6:18; Revelation 3:12.

10 Galatians 4:6.

11 Psalm 103:13; Proverbs 14:26; Matthew 6:32.

12 Hebrews 6:12.

13 1 Corinthians 6:11; Ephesians 1:4; 2 Thessalonians 2:13.

14 Romans 6:4-6.

15 Ephesians 4:23-24.

16 Acts 11:18; 1 John 3:9.

17 Ephesians 3:16-19; Colossians 1:10-11; Hebrews 6:11-12; Jude 20.

18 Romans 6:4,6,14; Galatians 5:24.

Q. 76. What is repentance to life?

A. Repentance to life is a saving grace,[1] accomplished in the heart of a sinner by the Spirit[2] and Word of God,[3] by which out of the sight and sense, not only of the danger,[4] but also of the filthiness and odiousness of his sins,[5] and upon the apprehension of God's mercy in Christ to such as are penitent,[6] he so grieves for,[7] and hates his sins,[8] as that he turns from them all to God,[9] desiring and endeavoring constantly to walk with Him in all the ways of new obedience.[10]

Q. 77. How do justification and sanctification differ?

A. Although sanctification is inseparably joined with justification,[11] they differ in that God, in justification, imputes the righteousness of Christ;[12] in sanctification, his Spirit infuses grace, and enables the exercise of it;[13] in the former, sin is pardoned;[14] in the other, it is subdued;[15] the one does equally free all believers from the revenging wrath of God, and that is accomplished perfectly in this life, that they never fall into condemnation;[16] the other is neither equal in all,[17] nor in this life perfect in any,[18] but growing up to perfection.[19]

Q. 78. From what arises the imperfection of sanctification in believers?

A. The imperfection of sanctification in believers arises from the remnants of sin in every part of them, and the perpetual lusting of the flesh against the Spirit; by which they are often foiled with temptations, and fall into many sins,[20] are hindered in all their spiritual service,[21] and their best works are imperfect and defiled in the sight of God.[22]

1   2 Timothy 2:25.
2   Zechariah 12:10.
3   Acts 11:18,20-21.
4   Ezekiel 18:28,30,32; Hosea 2:6-7;
    Luke 15:17-18.
5   Isaiah 30:22; Ezekiel 36:31.
6   Joel 2:12-13.
7   Jeremiah 31:18-19.
8   2 Corinthians 7:11.
9   1 Kings 8:8:47-48; Ezekiel 14:6; Acts 26:18.
10 2 Kings 23:25; Psalm 119:6,59,128; Luke 1:6.
11 1 Corinthians 1:30; 6:11.
12 Romans 4:6,8.
13 Ezekiel 36:27.
14 Romans 3:24-25.
15 Romans 6:6,14.
16 Romans 8:33-34.
17 Hebrews 5:12-14.; 1 John 2:12-14.
18 1 John 1:8,10.
19 2 Corinthians 7:1; Philippians 3:12-14.
20 Mark 14:66-72; Romans 7:18,23;
    Galatians 2:11-12,
21 Hebrews 12:1,
22 Exodus 28:38; Isaiah 64:6.

Q. 79.   May not true believers, by reason of their imperfections, and the many temptations and sins they are overtaken with, fall away from the state of grace?

A.   True believers, by reason of the unchangeable love of God,[1] and His decree and covenant to give them perseverance,[2] their inseparable union with Christ,[3] His continual intercession for them,[4] and the Spirit and seed of God remaining in them,[5] can neither totally nor finally fall away from the state of grace,[6] but are kept by the power of God through faith to salvation.[7]

Q. 80.   Can true believers be infallibly assured that they are in the estate of grace, and that they shall persevere in it to salvation?

A.   Such as truly believe in Christ, and endeavor to walk in all good conscience before Him,[8] may, without extraordinary revelation, by faith grounded on the truth of God's promises, and by the Spirit enabling them to discern in themselves those graces to which the promises of life are made,[9] and bearing witness with their spirits that they are the children of God,[10] be infallibly assured that they are in the estate of grace, and shall persevere in it to salvation.[11]

Q. 81.   Are all true believers at all times assured of their present being in the estate of grace, and that they shall be saved?

A.   Assurance of grace and salvation not being of the essence of faith,[12] true believers may wait long before they obtain it;[13] and, after the enjoyment thereof, may have it weakened and interrupted, through many disturbances, sins, temptations, and desertions;[14] yet are they never left without such a presence and support of the Spirit of God, as keeps them from sinking into utter despair.[15]

1   Jeremiah 31:3.
2   2 Samuel 23:5; 2 Timothy 2:19; Hebrews 13:20-21.
3   1 Corinthians 1:8-9.
4   Luke 22:32; Hebrews 7:25.
5   1 John 2:27; 3:9.
6   Jeremiah 32:40; John 10:28.
7   1 Peter 1:5.
8   1 John 2:3.
9   1 Corinthians 2:12; Hebrews 6:11-12; 1 John 3:14,18-19,21,24; 4:13,16.
10   Romans 8:16.
11   1 John 5:13.
12   Ephesians 1:13.
13   Psalm 88:1-3,6-7,9,10,13-15; Isaiah 50:10.
14   Psalm 22:1; 31:22; 51:8,12; 77:1-12; Song of Solomon 5:2-3,6.
15   Job 13:15; Psalm 73:15,23; Isaiah 54:7-10; 1 John 3:9.

Q. 82. What is the communion in glory that the members of the invisible church have with Christ?

A. The communion in glory that the members of the invisible church have with Christ, is in this life,[1] immediately after death,[2] and at last perfected at the resurrection and day of judgment.[3]

Q. 83. What is the communion in glory with Christ that the members of the invisible church enjoy in this life?

A. The members of the invisible church have communicated to them, in this life, the first fruits of glory with Christ, as they are members of Him their head, and so in Him have a share in the glory that He is fully possessed of;[4] and as a deposit on it, enjoy the sense of God's love,[5] peace of conscience, joy in the Holy Spirit, and hope of glory.[6] As, on the contrary, the sense of God's revenging wrath, horror of conscience, and a fearful expectation of judgment, are to the wicked the beginning of the torment that they shall endure after death.[7]

Q. 84. Shall all men die?

A. Death being threatened as the wages of sin,[8] it is appointed to all men once to die;[9] for that all have sinned.[10]

Q. 85. Death being the wages of sin, why are not the righteous delivered from death, seeing all their sins are forgiven in Christ?

A. The righteous shall be delivered from death itself at the last day, and even in death are delivered from the sting and curse of it;[11] so that although they die, yet it is out of God's love,[12] to free them perfectly from sin and misery,[13] and to make them capable of further communion with Christ in glory, which they then enter.[14]

1   2 Corinthians 3:18.
2   Luke 23:43.
3   1 Thessalonians 4:17.
4   Ephesians 2:5-6.
5   Romans 5:5; 2 Corinthians 1:22.
6   Romans 5:1-2; 14:17.
7   Genesis 4:13; Matthew 27:4; Mark 9:44; Romans 2:9; Hebrews 10:27.
8   Romans 6:23.
9   Hebrews 9:27.
10 Romans 5:12.
11 1 Corinthians 15:26,55-57; Hebrews 2:15.
12 2 Kings 22:20; Isaiah 57:1-2.
13 Ephesians 5:27; Revelation 14:13.
14 Luke 23:43.

Q. 86.   What is the communion in glory with Christ that the members of the invisible church enjoy immediately after death?

A.   The communion in glory with Christ that the members of the invisible church enjoy immediately after death, is that their souls are then made perfect in holiness,[1] and received into the highest heavens,[2] where they behold the face of God in light and glory;[3] waiting for the full redemption of their bodies,[4] which even in death continue united to Christ,[5] and rest in their graves as in their beds,[6] till at the last day they be again united to their souls.[7] Whereas the souls of the wicked are at their death cast into hell, where they remain in torments and utter darkness; and their bodies kept in their graves, as in their prisons, until the resurrection and judgment of the great day.[8]

Q. 87.   What are we to believe concerning the resurrection?

A.   We are to believe that, at the last day, there shall be a general resurrection of the dead, both of the just and unjust;[9] when they that are then found alive shall in a moment be changed; and the actual bodies of the dead that are laid in the grave, being then again united to their souls forever, shall be raised up by the power of Christ.[10] The bodies of the just, by the Spirit of Christ, and by virtue of his resurrection as their Head, shall be raised in power, spiritual, and incorruptible, and made like His glorious body:[11] and the bodies of the wicked shall be raised up in dishonor by Him as an offended judge.[12]

Q. 88.   What shall immediately follow after the resurrection?

A.   Immediately after the resurrection shall follow the general and final judgment of angels and men,[13] the day and hour of which no man knows, that all may watch and pray, and be ever ready for the coming of the Lord.[14]

---

1   Hebrews 12:32.
2   Acts 3:21; 2 Corinthians 5:1,6,8; Ephesians 4:10; Philippians 1:23.
3   1 Corinthians 13:12; 1 John 3:2.
4   Psalm 16:9; Romans 8:23.
5   1 Thessalonians 4:14.
6   Isaiah 57:2.
7   Job 19:26-27.
8   Luke 16:23-24; Acts 1:25; Jude 6-7.
9   Acts 24:15.
10   John 5:28-29; 1 Corinthians 15:51-53; 1 Thessalonians 4:15-17.
11   1 Corinthians 15:21-23,42-44; Philippians 3:21.
12   Matthew 25:33; John 5:27-29.
13   Matthew 25:46; 2 Peter 2:4,6-7,14-15.
14   Matthew 24:36,42,44.

Q. 89.   What shall be done to the wicked at the day of judgment?

A.   At the day of judgment, the wicked shall be set on Christ's left hand,[1] and upon clear evidence, and full conviction of their own consciences,[2] shall have the fearful but just sentence of condemnation pronounced against them;[3] and then shall be cast out from the favorable presence of God, and the glorious fellowship with Christ, His saints, and all His holy angels, into hell, to be punished with unspeakable torments both of body and soul, with the devil and his angels forever.[4]

Q. 90.   What shall be done to the righteous at the day of judgment?

A.   At the day of judgment, the righteous, being caught up to Christ in the clouds,[5] shall be set on his right hand, and, there openly acknowledged and acquitted,[6] shall join with Him in the judging of wicked angels and men;[7] and shall be received into heaven,[8] where they shall be fully and forever freed from all sin and misery;[9] filled with inconceivable joy;[10] made perfectly holy and happy both in body and soul, in the company of innumerable saints and angels,[11] but especially in the immediate vision and fruition of God the Father, of our Lord Jesus Christ, and of the Holy Spirit, to all eternity.[12] And this is the perfect and full communion that the members of the invisible church shall enjoy with Christ in glory, at the resurrection and day of judgment.

1   Matthew 25:33.
2   Romans 2:15-16.
3   Matthew 25:41-43.
4   Luke 16:26; 2 Thessalonians 1:8-9.
5   1 Thessalonians 4:17.
6   Matthew 10:32; 25:33.
7   1 Corinthians 6:2-3.

8   Matthew 25:34,46.
9   Ephesians 5:27; Revelation 14:13.
10 Psalm 16:11.
11 Hebrews 12:22-23.
12 1 Corinthians 13:12; 1 Thessalonians 4:17-18;
    1 John 3:2.

HAVING SEEN WHAT THE SCRIPTURES PRINCIPALLY TEACH US TO BELIEVE CONCERNING GOD, IT FOLLOWS TO CONSIDER WHAT THEY REQUIRE AS THE DUTY OF MAN

Q. 91. What is the duty that God requires of man?

A. The duty that God requires of man is obedience to his revealed will.[1]

Q. 92. What did God at first reveal to man as the rule of his obedience?

A. The rule of obedience revealed to Adam in the estate of innocence, and to all mankind in him, besides a special command, not to eat of the fruit of the Tree of the Knowledge of Good and Evil, was the moral law.[2]

Q. 93. What is the moral law?

A. The moral law is the declaration of the will of God to mankind, directing and binding everyone to personal, perfect, and perpetual conformity and obedience to it, in the frame and disposition of the whole man, soul and body,[3] and in performance of all those duties of holiness and righteousness that he owes to God and man:[4] promising life upon the fulfilling, and threatening death upon the breach of it.[5]

Q. 94. Is there any use of the moral law to man since the Fall?

A. Although no man since the Fall can attain to righteousness and life by the moral law,[6] yet there is great use for it, common to all men, as specific either to the unregenerate, or the regenerate.[7]

Q. 95. Of what use is the moral law to all men?

A. The moral law is of use to all men, to inform them of the holy nature and will of God,[8] and of their duty binding them to walk

---

1   1 Samuel 15:22; Micah 6:8; Romans 12:1-2.
2   Genesis 1:26-27; 2:17; Romans 2:14-15; 10:5.
3   Deuteronomy 5:1-3,31,33; Luke 10:26-27; Galatians 3:10; 1 Thessalonians 5:23.
4   Luke 1:75; Acts 24:16.
5   Romans 10:5; Galatians 3:10,13.
6   Romans 8:3; Galatians 2:16.
7   1 Timothy 1:8.
8   Leviticus 11:44-45; 20:7-8; Romans 8:12.

accordingly;[1] to convince them of their inability to keep it, and of the sinful pollution of their nature, hearts, and lives,[2] to humble them in the sense of their sin and misery,[3] and thereby help them to a clearer sight of the need they have of Christ,[4] and of the perfection of His obedience.[5]

Q. 96. What particular use is there of the moral law to unregenerate men?

A. The moral law is of use to unregenerate men, to awaken their consciences to flee from the wrath to come,[6] and to drive them to Christ;[7] or, upon their continuance in the estate and way of sin, to leave them inexcusable,[8] and under the curse of it.[9]

Q. 97. What special use is there of the moral law to the regenerate?

A. Although they who are regenerate and believe in Christ are delivered from the moral law as a Covenant of Works,[10] so as by it they are neither justified[11] nor condemned:[12] yet, besides the general uses of it common to them with all men, it is of special use to show them how much they are bound to Christ for his fulfilling it, and enduring the curse of it, in their place and for their good;[13] and thereby to provoke them to more thankfulness,[14] and to express the same in their greater care to conform themselves to it as the rule of their obedience.[15]

Q. 98. Where is the moral law found to be summarized?

A. The moral law is found summarized in the Ten Commandments, which were delivered by the voice of God on Mount Sinai, and written by Him on two tablets of stone;[16] and are recorded in the twentieth chapter of Exodus; the first four commandments containing our duty to God, and the other six our duty to man.[17]

1   Micah 6:8; James 2:10-11.
2   Psalm 19:11-12; Romans 3:20; 7:7.
3   Romans 3:9,23.
4   Galatians 3:21-22.
5   Romans 10:4.
6   1 Timothy 1:9-10.
7   Galatians 3:24.
8   Romans 1:20; 2:15.
9   Galatians 3:10.

10   Romans 6:14; 7:4,6; Galatians 4:4-5.
11   Romans 3:20.
12   Romans 8:1; Galatians 5:23.
13   Romans 7:24-25; 8:3-4; Galatians 3:13-14.
14   Luke 1:68-69,74-75; Colossians 1:12-14.
15   Romans 7:22; 12:2; Titus 2:11-14.
16   Exodus 34:1-4; Deuteronomy 10:4.
17   Matthew 22:37-40.

Q. 99. What rules are to be observed for the right understanding of the
Ten Commandments?

A. For the right understanding of the Ten Commandments, these
rules are to be observed:

1. That the law is perfect, and binds everyone to full conformity
in the whole man to the righteousness of it, and to entire
obedience forever; so as to require the utmost perfection of
every duty, and to forbid the least degree of every sin.[1]

2. That it is spiritual, and so reaches the understanding, will,
affections, and all other powers of the soul; as well as words,
works, and gestures.[2]

3. That one and the same thing, in various respects, is required
or forbidden in several commandments.[3]

4. That as, where a duty is commanded, the contrary sin is forbidden;[4] and where a sin is forbidden, the contrary duty is
commanded;[5] so, where a promise is attached, the contrary
threatening is included;[6] and where a threatening is attached,
the contrary promise is included.[7]

5. That what God forbids, is at no time to be done;[8] what he
commands is always our duty;[9] and yet every particular duty
is not to be done at all times.[10]

6. That, under one sin or duty, all of the same kind are forbidden or commanded; together with all the causes, means,
occasions, and appearances of it, and provocations to it.[11]

---

1   Psalm 19:7; Matthew 5:21-22; James 2:10.
2   Deuteronomy 6:5; Matthew 5:21-22,27-28,
33-34,37-39,43-44; 22:37-39; Romans 7:14.
3   Proverbs 1:19; Amos 8:5; Colossians 3:4; 1
Timothy 6:10.
4   Deuteronomy 6:13; Isaiah 58:13; Matthew
4:9-10; 15:4-6.
5   Matthew 5:21-25; Ephesians 4:28.
6   Exodus 20:12; Proverbs 30:17.

7   Exodus 20:7; Psalm 15:1,4-5; 24:4-5;
Jeremiah 18:7-8.
8   Job 13:7-8; 36:21; Romans 3:8;
Hebrews 11:25.
9   Deuteronomy 4:8-9.
10 Matthew 12:7.
11 Matthew 5:21-22,27-28; 15:4-6;
Galatians 5:26; Colossians 3:21;
1 Thessalonians 5:22; Hebrews 10:24-25;
Jude 23.

7. That what is forbidden or commanded to us, we are bound, according to our situations, to endeavor that it may be avoided or performed by others, according to the duty of their situations.[1]

8. That in what is commanded to others, we are bound, according to our situations and callings, to be helpful to them;[2] and to take heed of participating with others in what is forbidden them.[3]

Q. 100. What special things are we to consider in the Ten Commandments?

A. We are to consider in the Ten Commandments: the preface, the substances of the commandments themselves, and the several reasons attached to some of them to encourage greater enforcement of them.

Q. 101. What is the preface to the Ten Commandments?

A. The preface to the Ten Commandments is contained in these words: "I am the LORD your God, who brought you out of the land of Egypt, out of the house of slavery."[4] With this God makes known His sovereignty, as being Yahweh, the eternal, unchangeable, and almighty God;[5] having His existence in and of Himself,[6] and giving existence to all His words[7] and works;[8] and that He is a God in covenant, as with Israel of old, so with all His people;[9] who as He brought them out of their bondage in Egypt, so He delivered us from our spiritual bondage;[10] and that therefore we are bound to take Him for our God alone, and to keep all his commandments.[11]

1   Genesis 18:19; Exodus 20:10; Leviticus 19:17; Deuteronomy 6:6-7; Joshua 14:15.
2   2 Corinthians 1:24.
3   Ephesians 5:11; 1 Timothy 5:22.
4   Exodus 20:2 (English Standard Version).
5   Isaiah 44:6.
6   Exodus 3:14.
7   Exodus 6:3.
8   Acts 17:24,28.
9   Genesis 17:7; Romans 3:9.
10 Luke 1:74-75.
11 Leviticus 18:30; 19:37; 1 Peter 1:15,17-18.

Q. 102. What is the sum of the four commandments that contain our
duty to God?

A.　　　The sum of the four commandments containing our duty to
God is, to love the Lord our God with all our heart, and with all
our soul, and with all our strength, and with all our mind.[1]

Q. 103. Which is the First Commandment?

A.　　　The First Commandment is, "You shall have no other gods
before me."[2]

Q. 104. What are the duties required in the First Commandment?

A.　　　The duties required in the First Commandment are: the knowing and acknowledging of God to be the only true God, and
our God;[3] and to worship and glorify him accordingly;[4] by
thinking,[5] meditating,[6] remembering,[7] highly esteeming,[8] hon-
oring,[9] adoring,[10] choosing,[11] loving,[12] desiring,[13] fearing
him;[14] believing Him;[15] trusting,[16] hoping,[17] delighting,[18]
rejoicing in Him;[19] being zealous for Him;[20] calling upon Him,
giving all praise and thanks,[21] and yielding all obedience and
submission to Him with the whole man;[22] being careful in all
things to please Him,[23] and sorrowful when in anything He is
offended;[24] and walking humbly with Him.[25]

Q. 105. What are the sins forbidden in the First Commandment?

A.　　　The sins forbidden in the First Commandment are: atheism, in
denying or not having a God;[26] idolatry, in having or worshiping more gods than one, or any with, or instead of the true

1　Luke 10:27.
2　Exodus 20:3 (ESV)
3　Deuteronomy 26:7; 1 Chronicles 28:9;
　　Isaiah 43:10; Jeremiah 14:22.
4　Psalm 29:2; 95:6-7; Matthew 4:10.
5　Malachi 3:16.
6　Psalm 63:6.
7　Ecclesiastes 12:1.
8　Psalm 71:19.
9　Malachi 1:6.
10　Isaiah 45:23.
11　Joshua 24:15,22.
12　Deuteronomy 6:5.
13　Psalm 73:25.
14　Isaiah 8:13.
15　Exodus 14:31.
16　Isaiah 26:4.
17　Psalm 130:7.
18　Psalm 37:4.
19　Psalm 32:11.
20　Numbers 25:11; Romans 12:11.
21　Philippians 4:6.
22　Jeremiah 7:23; James 4:7.
23　1 John 3:22.
24　Psalm 119:136; Jeremiah 31:18.
25　Micah 6:8.
26　Psalm 14:1; Ephesians 2:12.

God;[1] the not having and acknowledging Him for God, and our God;[2] the omission or neglect of anything due to him, required in this commandment;[3] ignorance,[4] forgetfulness,[5] misunderstandings,[6] false opinions,[7] unworthy and wicked thoughts of Him;[8] bold and curious searchings into His secrets;[9] all profaneness,[10] hatred of God,[11] self-love,[12] self-seeking,[13] and all other inordinate and immoderate setting of our mind, will, or affections on other things, and taking them off Him in whole or in part;[14] vain gullibility,[15] unbelief,[16] heresy,[17] misbelief,[18] distrust,[19] despair,[20] incorrigibility,[21] and insensibility under judgments,[22] hardness of heart,[23] pride,[24] presumption,[25] carnal security,[26] tempting of God;[27] using unlawful means,[28] and trusting in lawful means;[29] carnal delights and joys,[30] corrupt, blind, and indiscreet zeal;[31] lukewarmness,[32] and deadness in the things of God;[33] estranging ourselves, and apostatizing from God;[34] praying or giving any religious worship to saints, angels, or any other creatures;[35] all compacts and consulting with the devil,[36] and listening to his suggestions;[37] making men the lords of our faith and conscience;[38] slighting and despising God, and His commands;[39] resisting and grieving of His Spirit,[40] discontent and impatience at His dispensations,

1 Jeremiah 2:27-28; 1 Thessalonians 1:9.
2 Psalm 81:11.
3 Isaiah 43:2,23-24.
4 Jeremiah 4:22; Hosea 4:1,6.
5 Jeremiah 2:32.
6 Acts 17:23,29.
7 Isaiah 40:18.
8 Psalm 50:21.
9 Deuteronomy 29:29.
10 Titus 1:16; Hebrews 12:16.
11 Romans 1:30.
12 2 Timothy 3:2.
13 Philippians 2:21.
14 1 Samuel 2:29; Colossians 2:2,5; 1 John 2:15-16.
15 1 John 4:1.
16 Hebrews 3:12.
17 Galatians 5:20; Titus 3:10.
18 Acts 26:9.
19 Psalm 78:22.
20 Genesis 4:13.
21 Jeremiah 5:3.
22 Isaiah 42:25.
23 Romans 2:5.
24 Jeremiah 13:15.
25 Psalm 10:13.
26 Zephaniah 1:12.
27 Matthew 4:7.
28 Romans 3:8.
29 Jeremiah 17:5.
30 2 Timothy 3:4.
31 Luke 9:54-55; John 16:2; Romans 10:2; Galatians 4:17.
32 Revelation 3:16.
33 Revelation 2:1.
34 Isaiah 1:4-5; Ezekiel 14:5.
35 Hosea 4:12; Matthew 4:10; Acts 10:25-26; Romans 1:25; 10:13-14; Colossians 2:18; Revelation 19:10.
36 Leviticus 20:6; 1 Samuel 28:7,11; 1 Chronicles 10:13-14.
37 Acts 5:3.
38 Matthew 23:9; 2 Corinthians 1:24.
39 Deuteronomy 32:15; 2 Samuel 12:9; Proverbs 13:13.
40 Acts 7:51; Ephesians 4:30.

charging Him foolishly for the evils He inflicts on us;[1] and ascribing the praise of any good that we are, have, or can do, to fortune,[2] idols,[3] ourselves,[4] or any other creature.[5]

Q. 106. What are we especially taught by the words "before me," in the First Commandment?

A. The words "before me," or "before my face," in the First Commandment, teach us, that God, who sees all things, takes special notice of, and is much displeased with, the sin of having any other God; so that it may be an argument to dissuade us from it, and to emphasize it as a most serious provocation;[6] as also to persuade us to do as in His sight, whatever we do in His service.[7]

Q. 107. Which is the Second Commandment?

A. The Second Commandment is, "You shall not make for yourself a carved image, or any likeness of anything that is in heaven above, or that is in the earth beneath, or that is in the water under the earth. You shall not bow down to them or serve them, for I the LORD your God am a jealous God, visiting the iniquity of the fathers on the children to the third and the fourth generation of those who hate me, but showing steadfast love to thousands of those who love me and keep my commandments."[8]

Q. 108. What are the duties required in the Second Commandment?

A. The duties required in the Second Commandment are: the receiving, observing, and keeping pure and entire, all such religious worship and ordinances as God has instituted in his Word;[9] particularly prayer and thanksgiving in the name of Christ;[10] the reading, preaching, and hearing of the Word;[11]

1   Job 1:22; Psalm 73:2-3,13-15,22.
2   1 Samuel 6:7-9.
3   Daniel 5:23.
4   Deuteronomy 8:17; Daniel 4:30.
5   Habakkuk 1:16.
6   Psalm 44:20-21; Ezekiel 8:5-6.
7   1 Chronicles 28:9.

8   Exodus 20:4-6 (ESV).
9   Deuteronomy 32:46-47; Matthew 28:20; Acts 2:42; 1 Timothy 6:13-14.
10 Ephesians 5:20; Philippians 4:6.
11 Deuteronomy 17:18-19; Acts 10:33; 15:21; 2 Timothy 4:2; James 1:21-22.

the administration and receiving of the sacraments;[1] church government and discipline;[2] the ministry and maintenance of them;[3] religious fasting;[4] swearing by the name of God;[5] and vowing to Him:[6] as also the disapproving, detesting, opposing all false worship;[7] and, according to each one's situation and calling, removing it, and all monuments of idolatry.[8]

Q. 109. What are the sins forbidden in the Second Commandment?

A.   The sins forbidden in the Second Commandment are: all developing,[9] counseling,[10] commanding,[11] using,[12] and in any way approving any religious worship not instituted by God Himself;[13] the making any representation of God, of all, or of any of the three Persons, either inwardly in our mind, or outwardly in any kind of image or likeness of any creature whatsoever;[14] all worshiping of it,[15] or God in it or by it;[16] the making of any representation of false deities,[17] and all worship of them, or service belonging to them;[18] all superstitious devices,[19] corrupting the worship of God,[20] adding to it, or taking from it,[21] whether invented and taken up of ourselves,[22] or received by tradition from others,[23] though under the title of antiquity,[24] custom,[25] devotion,[26] good intent, or any other pretense whatsoever;[27] buying or selling of pardons,[28] sacrilege;[29] all neglect,[30] contempt,[31] hindering,[32] and opposing the worship and ordinances that God has appointed.[33]

---

1   Matthew 28:19; 1 Corinthians 11:23-30.
2   Matthew 16:19: 18:15-17; 1 Corinthians 5; 12:28.
3   1 Corinthians 9:7-15; Ephesians 4:11-12; 1 Timothy 5:17-18.
4   Joel 2:12,18; 1 Corinthians 7:5.
5   Deuteronomy 6:13.
6   Psalm 76:11; Isaiah 19:21.
7   Psalm 16:4; Acts 17:16-17.
8   Deuteronomy 7:5; Isaiah 30:22.
9   Numbers 15:39.
10 Deuteronomy 13:6-8.
11 Hosea 5:11; Micah 6:16.
12 1 Kings 11:33; 12:33.
13 Deuteronomy 12:30-32.
14 Deuteronomy 4:15-19; Acts 17:29; Romans 1:21-23,25.
15 Daniel 3:18; Galatians 4:8.
16 Exodus 32:5.
17 Exodus 32:8.
18 1 Kings 18:26,28; Isaiah 65:11.
19 Acts 17:22; Colossians 2:21-23.
20 Malachi 1:7-6,14.
21 Deuteronomy 4:2.
22 Psalm 106:39.
23 Matthew 15:9.
24 1 Peter 1:8.
25 Jeremiah 44:17.
26 Isaiah 65:3-5; Galatians 1:13-14.
27 1 Samuel 13:11-12; 15:21.
28 Acts 8:18.
29 Malachi 3:8; Romans 2:22.
30 Exodus 4:24-26.
31 Malachi 1:7,13; Matthew 22:5.
32 Matthew 23:13.
33 Acts 13:44-45; 1 Thessalonians 2:15-16.

Q. 110. What are the reasons added to the Second Commandment, the more to enforce it?

A.　　The reasons added to the Second Commandment, the more to enforce it, contained in these words, "for I the LORD your God am a jealous God, visiting the iniquity of the fathers on the children to the third and the fourth generation of those who hate me, but showing steadfast love to thousands of those who love me and keep my commandments" [1] are, besides God's sovereignty over us, and ownership in us,[2] his fervent zeal for his own worship,[3] his revengeful indignation against all false worship, as being a spiritual prostitution;[4] accounting those who break this commandment such as hate him, and threatening to punish them for several generations,[5] and esteeming those who observe it as those who love him and keep his commandments, and promising mercy to them for many generations.[6]

Q. 111. Which is the Third Commandment?

A.　　The Third Commandment is, "You shall not take the name of the LORD your God in vain, for the LORD will not hold him guiltless who takes his name in vain."[7]

Q. 112. What is required in the Third Commandment?

A.　　The Third Commandment requires, that the name of God, His titles, attributes,[8] ordinances,[9] the Word,[10] sacraments,[11] prayer,[12] oaths,[13] vows,[14] casting of lots,[15] His works,[16] and whatever else there is by which he makes Himself known, be used in a holy and reverent manner in thought,[17] meditation,[18] word,[19] and writing;[20] by a holy profession,[21] and answerable

1　Exodus 20:5-6 (ESV).
2　Psalm 45:11; Revelation 15:3-4.
3　Exodus 34:13-14.
4　Deuteronomy 32:16-20; Jeremiah 7:18-20; Ezekiel 16:26-27; 1 Corinthians 10:20-22.
5　Hosea 2:2-4.
6　Deuteronomy 5:29.
7　Exodus 20:7 (ESV).
8　Deuteronomy 28:58; Psalm 29:2; 68:4; Matthew 11:9; Revelation 15:3-4.
9　Ecclesiastes 5:1; Malachi 1:14.
10　Psalm 138:2.
11　1 Corinthians 11:24-25,28-29.
12　1 Timothy 2:8.
13　Jeremiah 4:2.
14　Ecclesiastes 5:2-6.
15　Acts 1:24,26.
16　Job 36:24.
17　Malachi 3:16.
18　Psalm 8:1,3-4,9.
19　Psalm 105:2,5; Colossians 3:17.
20　Psalm 102:18.
21　Micah 4:5; 1 Peter 3:15.

conversation[1] to the glory of God,[2] and the good of ourselves[3] and others.[4]

Q. 113. What are the sins forbidden in the Third Commandment?

A. The sins forbidden in the Third Commandment are: the failure to use God's name as is required;[5] and the abuse of it in an ignorant,[6] vain,[7] irreverent, profane,[8] superstitious,[9] or wicked mentioning or otherwise using the titles, attributes,[10] ordinances,[11] or works;[12] by blasphemy;[13] perjury;[14] all sinful cursing,[15] oaths,[16] vows,[17] and casting of lots;[18] violating our oaths and vows, if lawful;[19] and fulfilling them, if of things unlawful;[20] murmuring and quarreling at,[21] curious prying into,[22] and misapplying of God's decrees[23] and providence;[24] misinterpreting,[25] misapplying,[26] or any way perverting the Word, or any part of it,[27] to profane jokes,[28] curious and unprofitable questions, vain discord, or the maintaining of false doctrines;[29] abusing it, the creatures, or anything contained under the name of God, to charms,[30] or sinful lusts and practices;[31] the maligning,[32] scorning,[33] verbally abusing,[34] or any way opposing of God's truth, grace, and ways;[35] making profession of religion in hypocrisy, or for sinister ends;[36] being ashamed of it,[37] or a shame to it, by uncomfortable,[38] unwise,[39] unfruitful,[40] and offensive departing[41] or backsliding from it.[42]

1 Philippians 1:27.
2 1 Corinthians 10:31.
3 Jeremiah 32:39.
4 1 Peter 2:12.
5 Malachi 2:2.
6 Acts 17:23.
7 Proverbs 30:9.
8 Malachi 1:6-6,12; 3:14.
9 1 Samuel 4:3-5; Jeremiah 7:4,9-10,14,31; Colossians 2:20-22.
10 Exodus 5:2; 2 Kings 18:30,35; Psalm 139:20.
11 Psalm 50:16-17.
12 Isaiah 5:12.
13 Leviticus 24:11; 2 Kings 19:22.
14 Zechariah 5:4; 8:17.
15 1 Samuel 17:43; 2 Samuel 16:5.
16 Jeremiah 5:7; 23:10.
17 Deuteronomy 23:18; Acts 23:12,14.
18 Esther 3:7; 9:24; Psalm 22:18.
19 Psalm 4:4; Ezekiel 17:16,18-19.
20 Mark 6:26; 1 Samuel 25:22,32-34.
21 Romans 9:14,19-20.
22 Deuteronomy 29:29.
23 Romans 3:5-7; 6:1.
24 Psalm 39; Ecclesiastes 8:11; 9:3.
25 Matthew 5:21-48.
26 Ezekiel 13:22.
27 Matthew 22:23-32; 2 Peter 3:16.
28 Isaiah 22:13; Jeremiah 23:34,36,38.
29 1 Timothy 1:4,6-7; 6:4-5,20; 2 Timothy 2:14; Titus 3:9.
30 Deuteronomy 18:10-13; Acts 19:13.
31 1 Kings 21:9-10; Romans 13:13-14; 2 Timothy 4:3-4; Jude 4.
32 Acts 13:45; 1 John 3:12.
33 Psalm 1:1; 2 Peter 3:3.
34 1 Peter 4:4.
35 Acts 4:18; 13:45-46,50; 19:9; 1 Thessalonians 2:16; Hebrews 10:29.
36 Matthew 6:1-2,5,16; 23:14; 2 Timothy 3:5.
37 Mark 8:38.
38 Psalm 73:14-15.
39 1 Corinthians 6:5-6; Ephesians 5:15-17.
40 Isaiah 5:4; 2 Peter 1:8-9.
41 Romans 2:23-24.
42 Galatians 3:1,3; Hebrews 6:6.

Q. 114. What reasons are attached to the Third Commandment?

A.   The reasons attached to the Third Commandment, in the words, "the Lord your God," and, "for the LORD will not hold him guiltless who takes his name in vain,"[1] are because He is the Lord and our God, therefore his name is not to be profaned, or any way abused by us;[2] especially because he will be so far from acquitting and sparing the transgressors of this commandment, as that he will not suffer them to escape his righteous judgment,[3] even though many of them escape the censures and punishments of men.[4]

Q. 115. Which is the Fourth Commandment?

A.   The Fourth Commandment is, "Remember the Sabbath day, to keep it holy. Six days you shall labor, and do all your work, but the seventh day is a Sabbath to the LORD your God. On it you shall not do any work, you, or your son, or your daughter, your male servant, or your female servant, or your livestock, or the sojourner who is within your gates. For in six days the LORD made heaven and earth, the sea, and all that is in them, and rested the seventh day. Therefore the LORD blessed the Sabbath day and made it holy."[5]

Q. 116. What is required in the Fourth Commandment?

A.   The Fourth Commandment requires of all men the sanctifying or keeping holy to God such set times as He has appointed in His Word, expressly one whole day in seven; which was the seventh from the beginning of the world to the resurrection of Christ, and the first day of the week ever since, and so to continue to the end of the world; which is the Christian Sabbath,[6] and in the New Testament called "the Lord's Day."[7]

Q. 117. How is the Sabbath or Lord's Day to be sanctified?

A.   The Sabbath, or Lord's Day, is to be sanctified by a holy resting all that day,[8] not only from such works as are at all times sinful, but even from such worldly employments and recreations as

1   Exodus 20:7 (ESV).
2   Leviticus 19:12.
3   Deuteronomy 28:58-59; Ezekiel 36:21-23; Zechariah 5:2-4.
4   1 Samuel 2:12,17,22,24; 3:13.
5   Exodus 20:8-11 (ESV).
6   Genesis 2:2-3; Deuteronomy 5:12-14; Isaiah 56:2,4,6-7; Matthew 5:17-18; 1 Corinthians 16:1-2.
7   Revelation 1:10.
8   Exodus 20:8,10.

are on other days lawful;[1] and making it our delight to spend the whole time (except so much of it as is to be taken up in works of necessity and mercy)[2] in the public and private exercise of God's worship.[3] And, to that end, we are to prepare our hearts, and with such foresight, diligence, and moderation, to arrange, and to accomplish ahead of time our worldly business, that we may be the more free and prepared for the duties of the day.[4]

Q. 118. Why is the responsibility of keeping the Sabbath more particularly directed to heads of families and other superiors?

A. The responsibility of keeping the Sabbath is more particularly directed to heads of families and other superiors, because they are bound not only to keep it themselves, but to see that it is observed by all those who are under their charge; and because they are prone often to hinder them by employments of their own.[5]

Q. 119. What are the sins forbidden in the Fourth Commandment?

A. The sins in the Fourth Commandment are: all omissions of the duties required,[6] all careless, negligent, and unprofitable performing of them, and being weary of them;[7] all profaning the day by idleness, and doing that which is in itself sinful;[8] and by all needless works, words, and thoughts about our worldly employments and recreations.[9]

Q. 120. What are the reasons attached to the Fourth Commandment, the more to enforce it?

A. The reasons attached to the Fourth Commandment, the more to enforce it, are taken from the principles of it, God allowing us six days of seven for our own affairs, and reserving but one for Himself, in the words, "Six days you shall labor, and do all

---

1 Exodus 16:25-28; Nehemiah 13:15-22; Jeremiah 17:21-22.
2 Matthew 11:1-13.
3 Leviticus 23:3; Psalm 92 (title); Isaiah 58:18; 66:23; Luke 4:16; Acts 20:7; 1 Corinthians 16:1-2.
4 Exodus 16:22,25-26,29; 20:8,56; Nehemiah 13:19-22.

5 Exodus 20:10; 23:12; Joshua 24:15; Nehemiah 13:15,17; Jeremiah 17:20-22.
6 Ezekiel 22:26.
7 Ezekiel 33:30-32; Amos 8:5; Malachi 1:13; Acts 20:7,9.
8 Ezekiel 23:38.
9 Isaiah 58:13; Jeremiah 17:24,27.

your work"[1]; from God's establishment of a special ownership in that day with the words, "the seventh day is a Sabbath to the LORD your God"[2] from the example of God who "in six days … made heaven and earth, the sea, and all that is in them, and rested the seventh day"; and from the blessing that God put on the day, not only in sanctifying it to be a holy day for His service, but in ordaining it to be a means of blessing to us in our sanctifying it, "Therefore the LORD blessed the Sabbath day and made it holy."[3]

Q. 121. Why is the word "remember" set in the beginning of the Fourth Commandment?

A. The word "remember" is set in the beginning of the Fourth Commandment,[4] partly because of the great benefit of remembering it, we being thereby helped in our preparation to keep it;[5] and, in keeping it, better at keeping the rest of the commandments[6] and to continue a thankful remembrance of the two great benefits of creation and redemption, which contain an abridged picture of religion:[7] and partly because we are ready to forget it,[8] for that there is less light of nature for it, and yet it restrains our natural liberty in things at other times lawful;[9] that it comes but once in seven days, and many worldly businesses come between, and too often take our minds away from thinking of it, either to prepare for it, or to sanctify it;[10] and that Satan with his followers try hard to blot out the glory, and even the memory of it, and to bring in all hostility to religion and lack of respect for it.[11]

Q. 122. What is the sum of the six commandments that contain our duty to man?

A. The sum of the six commandments that contain our duty to man is, to love our neighbor as ourselves,[12] and to do to others what we would have them to do to us.[13]

---

1   Exodus 20:9 (ESV).
2   Exodus 20:10 (ESV).
3   Exodus 20:11 (ESV).
4   Exodus 20:8.
5   Exodus 16:23; Nehemiah 13:19; Mark 15:42;
    Luke 23:54,56.
6   Psalm 92:13-14; Ezekiel 20:12,19-20.
7   Genesis 2:2-3; Psalm 118:22,24; Acts 4:10-11;
    Revelation 1:10.
8   Ezekiel 22:26.
9   Nehemiah 9:14.
10 Deuteronomy 5:14-15; Amos 8:5.
11 Nehemiah 13:15-23; Jeremiah 17:21-23;
    Lamentations 1:7.
12 Matthew 22:39.
13 Matthew 7:12.

Q. 123. Which is the Fifth Commandment?

A.   The Fifth Commandment is, "Honor your father and your mother, that your days may be long in the land that the LORD your God is giving you."[1]

Q. 124. Who are meant by "father" and "mother," in the Fifth Commandment?

A.   By "father" and "mother" in the Fifth Commandment, are meant not only natural parents,[2] but all superiors in age[3] and giftedness;[4] and especially such as by God's ordinance are over us in place of authority, whether in family,[5] church,[6] or government.[7]

Q. 125. Why are superiors styled "father" and "mother"?

A.   Superiors are styled "father" and "mother" both to teach them in all duties toward their inferiors, as with natural parents, to express love and tenderness to them, according to their various relationships,[8] and to work inferiors to a greater willingness and cheerfulness in performing their duties to their superiors, as to their parents.[9]

Q. 126. What is the general scope of the Fifth Commandment?

A.   The general scope of the Fifth Commandment is, the performance of those duties that we mutually owe in our various relationships, as inferiors, superiors, or equals.[10]

Q. 127. What is the honor that inferiors owe to superiors?

A.   The honor that inferiors owe to their superiors is: all due reverence in heart,[11] word,[12] and behavior;[13] prayer and thanksgiving for them;[14] imitation of their virtues and graces;[15] willing obedience to their lawful commands and counsels,[16] due

1   Exodus 20:12 (ESV).
2   Proverbs 23:22,25; Ephesians 6:1.
3   1 Timothy 5:1-2.
4   Genesis 4:20-22; 45:8.
5   2 Kings 5:13.
6   2 Kings 2:12; 13:14; Galatians 4:19.
7   Isaiah 49:23.
8   Numbers 11:11-12; 2 Corinthians 12:14; Ephesians 6:4; 1 Thessalonians 2:7-8,11.
9   2 Kings 5:13; 1 Corinthians 4:14-16.
10 Romans 12:10; Ephesians 5:21; 1 Peter 2:17.
11 Leviticus 19:3; Malachi 1:6.
12 Proverbs 31:28; 1 Peter 3:6.
13 Leviticus 19:32; 1 Kings 2:19.
14 1 Timothy 2:1-2.
15 Philippians 3:17; Hebrews 13:7.
16 Exodus 18:19,24; Proverbs 4:3-4; 23:22; Romans 13:1-5; Ephesians 6:1-2,6-7; Hebrews 13:17; 1 Peter 2:13-14.

submission to their corrections;[1] fidelity to,[2] defense[3] and maintenance of them and their authority, according to their various ranks, and the nature of their situations;[4] bearing with their infirmities, and covering them in love,[5] so that they may be an honor to them and to their government.[6]

Q. 128. What are the sins of inferiors against their superiors?

A. The sins of inferiors against their superiors are: all neglect of the duties required toward them;[7] envying at,[8] contempt of,[9] and rebellion[10] against them[11] and their status,[12] in their lawful counsels,[13] commands, and corrections;[14] cursing, mocking,[15] and all such obstinate and scandalous posturing, as proves a shame and dishonor to them and their government.[16]

Q. 129. What is required of superiors toward their inferiors?

A. It is required of superiors, according to that power they receive from God, and that relationship in which they stand, to love,[17] pray for,[18] and bless their inferiors;[19] to instruct,[20] counsel, and admonish them;[21] supporting,[22] commending,[23] and rewarding such as do well;[24] and withholding support,[25] rebuking, and chastising such as do ill;[26] protecting,[27] and providing for them all things necessary for soul[28] and body;[29] and, by grave, wise, holy, and exemplary posture, to obtain glory to God,[30] honor to themselves,[31] and so to preserve the authority that God has put on them.[32]

1   Hebrews 12:9; 1 Peter 2:18-20.
2   Titus 2:9-10.
3   1 Samuel 26:15-16; 2 Samuel 18:3; Esther 6:2.
4   Genesis 45:11; 47:12; Matthew 22:21; Romans 13:6-7; Galatians 6:6; 1 Timothy 5:17-18.
5   Genesis 9:23; Proverbs 23:22; 1 Peter 2:18.
6   Proverbs 31:23; Psalm 127:3-5.
7   Matthew 15:4-6.
8   Numbers 11:28-29.
9   1 Samuel 8:7.
10 2 Samuel 15:1-12.
11 Exodus 24:15.
12 1 Samuel 10:27.
13 1 Samuel 2:25.
14 Deuteronomy 21:18-21.
15 Proverbs 30:11,17.
16 Proverbs 19:26.
17 Colossians 3:19; Titus 2:4.
18 Job 1:5; 1 Samuel 12:23.
19 Genesis 49:28; 1 Kings 8:55-56; Hebrews 7:7.
20 Deuteronomy 6:6-7.
21 Ephesians 6:4.
22 1 Peter 3:7.
23 Romans 13:3; 1 Peter 2:14.
24 Esther 6:3.
25 Romans 13:3-4.
26 Proverbs 29:15; 1 Peter 2:14.
27 Job 29:13-16; Isaiah 1:10,17.
28 Ephesians 6:4.
29 1 Timothy 5:8.
30 1 Timothy 4:12; Titus 2:3-5.
31 1 Kings 3:28.
32 Titus 2:15.

Q. 130. What are the sins of superiors?

A.   The sins of superiors are, besides the neglect of the duties required
       of them,[1] an inordinate seeking of themselves,[2] their own
       glory,[3] ease, profit, or pleasure;[4] commanding things unlawful,[5]
       or not in the power of inferiors to perform;[6] counseling,[7]
       encouraging,[8] or favoring them in that which is evil;[9] dissuad-
       ing, discouraging, or withholding support for them in that which
       is good;[10] correcting them unnecessarily;[11] carelessly exposing
       or leaving them to wrong, temptation, and danger;[12] provoking
       them to wrath;[13] or any way dishonoring themselves, or lessen-
       ing their authority, by an unjust, indiscreet, rigorous, or negli-
       gent behavior.[14]

Q. 131. What are the duties of equals?

A.   The duties of equals are: to regard the dignity and worth of each
       other,[15] in giving honor to go before one another,[16] and to rejoice
       in each other's giftedness and advancement as their own.[17]

Q. 132. What are the sins of equals?

A.   The sins of equals are, besides the neglect of the duties
       required,[18] the undervaluing of the worth,[19] envying the gifted-
       ness,[20] grieving at the advancement or prosperity of the other,[21]
       and seizing superiority over the other.[22]

Q. 133. What is the reason attached to the Fifth Commandment, the
        more to enforce it?

A.   The reason attached to the Fifth Commandment in these words,
       "that your days may be long in the land that the LORD your

---

1   Ezekiel 34:2-4.
2   Philippians 2:21.
3   John 5:44; 7:18.
4   Deuteronomy 17:17; Isaiah 56:10-11.
5   Daniel 3:4-6; Acts 4:17-18.
6   Exodus 5:10-18; Matthew 23:2,4.
7   Matthew 14:8; Mark 6:24.
8   2 Samuel 13:28.
9   1 Samuel 3:13.
10 Exodus 5:17; John 7:46-49; Colossians 3:21.
11 Deuteronomy 25:3; Hebrews 12:10;
    1 Peter 2:18-20.
12 Genesis 38:11,26; Acts 18:17.
13 Ephesians 6:4.
14 Genesis 9:21; 1 Samuel 2:29-31; 1 Kings 1:6;
    12:13-16.
15 1 Peter 2:17.
16 Romans 12:10.
17 Romans 12:15-16; Philippians 2:3-4.
18 Romans 13:8.
19 2 Timothy 3:3.
20 Acts 7:9; Galatians 5:26.
21 Numbers 12:2; Esther 6:12-13.
22 Luke 22:24; 3 John 9.

God is giving you,"[1] is an express promise of long life and prosperity, as far as it shall serve for God's glory and their own good, to all such as keep this commandment.[2]

Q. 134. Which is the Sixth Commandment?

A. The Sixth Commandment is, "You shall not murder."[3]

Q. 135. What are the duties required in the Sixth Commandment?

A. The duties required in the Sixth Commandment are: all careful studies and lawful endeavors, to preserve the lives of ourselves[4] and others,[5] by resisting all thoughts and purposes,[6] subduing all passions,[7] and avoiding all occasions,[8] temptations,[9] and practices that tend to the unjust taking away the life of any;[10] by just defense of life against violence;[11] patient bearing of the hand of God,[12] quietness of mind,[13] cheerfulness of spirit;[14] a sober use of meat,[15] drink,[16] medicine,[17] sleep,[18] labor,[19] and recreation;[20] by charitable thoughts,[21] love,[22] compassion,[23] meekness, gentleness, kindness;[24] peaceable,[25] mild, and courteous speech and behavior,[26] restraint, readiness to be reconciled, patient bearing and forgiving of injuries, and repaying good for evil;[27] comforting and relieving the distressed, and protecting and defending the innocent.[28]

Q. 136. What are the sins forbidden in the Sixth Commandment?

A. The sins forbidden in the Sixth Commandment are: all taking away of the lives of ourselves,[29] or of others,[30] except in case of public justice,[31] lawful war,[32] or necessary defense;[33] the

1 Exodus 20:12 (ESV).
2 Deuteronomy 5:16; 1 Kings 8:25; Ephesians 6:2-3.
3 Exodus 20:13 (ESV).
4 Ephesians 5:28-29.
5 1 Kings 18:4.
6 Jeremiah 26:15-16; Acts 23:12,16-17,21,27.
7 Ephesians 4:26-27.
8 Deuteronomy 22:8; 2 Samuel 2:22.
9 Proverbs 1:10,11,15-16; Matthew 4:6-7.
10 Genesis 37:21-22; 1 Samuel 24:12; 26:9-11.
11 1 Samuel 14:45; Psalm 82:4; Proverbs 24:11-12.
12 Hebrews 12:9; James 5:7-11.
13 Psalm 37:8-11; 1 Thessalonians 4:11; 1 Peter 3:3-4.
14 Proverbs 17:22.
15 Proverbs 25:16,27.
16 1 Timothy 5:23.
17 Isaiah 38:21.
18 Psalm 127:2.
19 Proverbs 16:20; Ecclesiastes 5:12; 2 Thessalonians 3:10,12.
20 Ecclesiastes 3:4,11.
21 1 Samuel 19:4-5; 22:13-14.
22 Romans 13:10.
23 Luke 10:33-34.
24 Colossians 3:12-13.
25 James 3:17.
26 Judges 8:1-3; Proverbs 15:1; 1 Peter 3:8-11.
27 Matthew 5:24; Romans 12:17,20; Ephesians 5:2,32.
28 Job 31:19-20; Proverbs 31:8-9; Matthew 25:35-36; 1 Thessalonians 5:14.
29 Acts 16:28.
30 Genesis 9:6.
31 Numbers 35:31,33.
32 Deuteronomy 20:1; Jeremiah 48:10.
33 Exodus 22:2-3.

neglecting or withdrawing of the lawful or necessary means of preservation of life;[1] sinful anger,[2] hatred,[3] envy,[4] desire for revenge;[5] all excessive passions;[6] distracting cares;[7] immoderate use of meat, drink,[8] labor,[9] and recreation;[10] provoking words;[11] oppression,[12] quarreling,[13] striking, wounding,[14] and whatever else tends to the destruction of the life of anyone.[15]

Q. 137. Which is the Seventh Commandment?

A. The Seventh Commandment is, "You shall not commit adultery."[16]

Q. 138. What are the duties required in the Seventh Commandment?

A. The duties required in the Seventh Commandment are: chastity in body, mind, affections,[17] words,[18] and behavior,[19] and the preservation of it in ourselves and others;[20] watchfulness over the eyes and all the senses;[21] temperance,[22] keeping of chaste company,[23] modesty in apparel,[24] marriage by those who do not have the gift of self-restraint,[25] marital love,[26] and cohabitation;[27] diligent labor in our callings;[28] shunning of all occasions of unchastity, and resisting temptations to it.[29]

Q. 139. What are the sins forbidden in the Seventh Commandment?

A. The sins forbidden in the Seventh Commandment, besides the neglect of the duties required,[30] are: adultery, fornication,[31] rape, incest,[32] sodomy, and all unnatural lusts;[33] all unclean imaginations, thoughts, purposes, and affections;[34] all corrupt

1   Ecclesiastes 6:1-2; Matthew 25:42-43; James 2:15-16.
2   Matthew 5:22.
3   Leviticus 19:17; 1 John 3:15.
4   Proverbs 14:30.
5   Romans 12:19.
6   Ephesians 4:31.
7   Matthew 6:31,34.
8   Luke 21:34; Romans 13:13.
9   Ecclesiastes 2:22-23; 12:12.
10 Isaiah 5:12.
11 Proverbs 12:18; 15:1.
12 Exodus 1:14; Ezekiel 18:18.
13 Proverbs 23:29; Galatians 5:15.
14 Numbers 35:16-18,21.
15 Exodus 21:18-36.
16 Exodus 20:14 (ESV).
17 Job 31:1; 1 Corinthians 7:34; 1 Thessalonians 4:4.
18 Colossians 4:6.
19 1 Peter 2:3.
20 1 Corinthians 7:2,35-36.
21 Job 31:1.
22 Acts 24:24-25.
23 Proverbs 2:16-20.
24 1 Timothy 2:9.
25 1 Corinthians 7:2,9.
26 Proverbs 5:19-20.
27 1 Peter 3:7.
28 Proverbs 3:11,27-28.
29 Genesis 39:8-10; Proverbs 5:8.
30 Proverbs 5:7.
31 Galatians 5:19; Hebrews 13:4.
32 2 Samuel 13:14; 1 Corinthians 5:1.
33 Leviticus 20:15-16; Romans 1:24,26-27.
34 Matthew 5:28; 15:19; Colossians 3:5.

or filthy communications, or listening to them;[1] lewd looks,[2] impudent or light behavior, immodest apparel,[3] prohibiting of lawful,[4] and dispensing with unlawful marriages;[5] allowing, tolerating, keeping of houses of prostitution, and patronizing them;[6] entangling vows of single life,[7] undue delay of marriage;[8] having more wives or husbands than one at the same time;[9] unjust divorce[10] or desertion;[11] idleness, gluttony, drunkenness,[12] unchaste company;[13] lascivious songs, books, pictures, dances, theater,[14] and all other provocations to, or acts of, uncleanness either in ourselves or others.[15]

Q. 140. Which is the Eighth Commandment?

A.   The Eighth Commandment is, "You shall not steal."[16]

Q. 141. What are the duties required in the Eighth Commandment?

A.   The duties required in the Eighth Commandment are: truth, faithfulness, and justice in contracts and commerce between man and man;[17] restitution of goods unlawfully detained from the right owners of them;[18] giving and lending freely, according to our abilities, and the needs of others;[19] moderation of our judgments, wills, and affections, concerning worldly goods;[20] a provident care and study to get,[21] keep, use, and dispose of those things that are necessary and convenient for the support of our nature, and suitable to our condition;[22] a lawful calling,[23] and a diligence in it;[24] frugality;[25] avoiding unnecessary

1   Proverbs 7:5,21-22; Ephesians 5:3-4.
2   Isaiah 3:16; 2 Peter 2:14.
3   Proverbs 7:10,13.
4   1 Timothy 4:3.
5   Leviticus 18:1-21; Malachi 2:11-12; Mark 6:18.
6   Leviticus 19:29; Deuteronomy 23:17-18; 1 Kings 15:12; 2 Kings 23:7; Proverbs 7:24-27; Jeremiah 5:7.
7   Matthew 19:10-11.
8   Genesis 38:26; 1 Corinthians 7:7-9.
9   Malachi 2:14-15; Matthew 19:5.
10   Malachi 2:16; Matthew 5:32.
11   1 Corinthians 7:12-13.
12   Proverbs 23:30-33; Ezekiel 16:49.
13   Genesis 39:19; Proverbs 5:8.
14   Isaiah 3:16; 23:15-17; Ezekiel 23:14-16; Mark 6:22; Romans 13:13; Ephesians 5:4; 1 Peter 4:3.
15   2 Kings 9:30; Jeremiah 4:30; Ezekiel 23:40.
16   Exodus 20:15 (ESV).
17   Psalm 15:2,4; Zechariah 7:4,10; 8:16-17.
18   Leviticus 6:2-5; Luke 19:8.
19   Luke 6:30,38; Galatians 6:10; Ephesians 4:28; 1 John 3:17.
20   Galatians 6:14; 1 Timothy 6:6-9.
21   1 Timothy 5:8.
22   Proverbs 27:23-27; Ecclesiastes 2:24; 3:12-13; Isaiah 38:1; Matthew 11:8; 1 Timothy 6:17-18.
23   Genesis 2:15; 3:19; 1 Corinthians 7:20.
24   Proverbs 10:4; Ephesians 4:28.
25   Proverbs 21:20; John 6:12.

lawsuits,[1] and pledge of security, or other like engagements;[2] and an endeavor by all just and lawful means to obtain, preserve, and further the wealth and outward estate of others, as well as our own.[3]

Q. 142. What are the sins forbidden in the Eighth Commandment?

A. The sins forbidden in the Eighth Commandment, besides the neglect of duties required,[4] are: theft,[5] robbery,[6] man-stealing,[7] and receiving anything that is stolen;[8] fraudulent dealing,[9] false weights and measures,[10] removing property markers,[11] injustice and unfaithfulness in contracts between man and man,[12] or in matters of trust;[13] oppression,[14] extortion,[15] usury,[16] bribery,[17] frivolous lawsuits,[18] unjust confinement and forced migration or genocide;[19] gaining a monopoly on commodities to enhance the price,[20] unlawful callings,[21] and all other unjust or sinful ways of taking or withholding from our neighbor what belongs to him, or of enriching ourselves;[22] covetousness,[23] inordinate prizing of and affection for worldly goods;[24] distrustful and distracting cares and studies in getting, keeping, and using them;[25] envying of the prosperity of others;[26] as likewise idleness,[27] extravagance, wasteful gaming, and all other ways by which we do unnecessarily risk our own outward estate;[28] and defrauding ourselves of the due use and comfort of the estate that God has given us.[29]

---

1   1 Corinthians 6:1-9.
2   Proverbs 6:1-6; 11:15.
3   Genesis 47:14,20; Exodus 23:4-5; Leviticus 24:35; Deuteronomy 22:1-4; Matthew 22:39; Philippians 2:4.
4   James 2:15-16; 1 John 3:17.
5   Ephesians 4:28.
6   Psalm 62:10.
7   1 Timothy 1:10.
8   Psalm 50:18; Proverbs 29:24.
9   1 Thessalonians 4:6.
10 Proverbs 11:1; 20:10.
11 Deuteronomy 19:14; Proverbs 23:10.
12 Psalm 37:21; Amos 8:5.
13 Luke 16:10-12.
14 Leviticus 25:17; Ezekiel 22:29.

15 Ezekiel 22:12; Matthew 23:25.
16 Psalm 15:5.
17 Job 15:34.
18 Proverbs 3:29-30; 1 Corinthians 6:6-8.
19 Isaiah 5:8; Micah 2:2.
20 Proverbs 11:26.
21 Acts 19:19,24-25.
22 Job 20:19; Proverbs 21:6; James 5:4.
23 Luke 12:15.
24 Psalm 62:10; Proverbs 23:5; Colossians 3:2; 1 Timothy 6:5.
25 Ecclesiastes 5:12; Matthew 6:25,31,34.
26 Psalm 37:1,7; 73:3.
27 Proverbs 18:9; 2 Thessalonians 3:11.
28 Proverbs 21:17; 23:20-21; 28:19.
29 Ecclesiastes 4:8; 6:2; 1 Timothy 5:8.

Q. 143. Which is the Ninth Commandment?

A.   The Ninth Commandment is, "You shall not bear false witness against your neighbor."[1]

Q. 144. What are the duties required in the Ninth Commandment?

A.   The duties required in the Ninth Commandment are: the preserving and promoting of truth between man and man,[2] and the good name of our neighbor, as well as our own;[3] appearing and standing for the truth;[4] and from the heart,[5] sincerely,[6] freely,[7] clearly,[8] and fully,[9] speaking the truth, and only the truth, in matters of judgment and justice,[10] and in all other things whatsoever;[11] a charitable esteem of our neighbors, [12] loving, desiring, and rejoicing in their good name;[13] sorrowing for,[14] and covering of their infirmities;[15] freely acknowledging of their gifts and graces,[16] defending their innocence;[17] a ready receiving of good report,[18] and unwillingness to admit of an evil report concerning them;[19] discouraging gossips,[20] flatterers,[21] and slanderers;[22] love and care of our own good name, and defending it when necessary;[23] keeping of lawful promises;[24] studying and practicing of whatever things are true, honest, lovely, and of good report.[25]

Q. 145. What are the sins forbidden in the Ninth Commandment?

A.   The sins forbidden in the Ninth Commandment are: all premature judging of the truth, and the good name of our neighbors as well as our own,[26] especially in public administration of justice;[27] giving false evidence,[28] inducing of false witnesses,[29]

1   Exodus 20:16 (ESV).
2   Zachariah 8:16.
3   3 John 12.
4   Proverbs 31:8-9.
5   Psalm 15:2.
6   2 Chronicles 19:9.
7   1 Samuel 19:4-5.
8   Joshua 7:19.
9   2 Samuel 14:18-20.
10   Leviticus 19:15; Proverbs 14:5,25.
11   2 Corinthians 1:17-18; Ephesians 4:25.
12   1 Corinthians 13:7; Hebrews 6:9.
13   Romans 1:8; 2 John 4; 3 John 3-4.
14   2 Corinthians 2:4; 12:21.
15   Proverbs 17:9; 1 Peter 4:8.
16   1 Corinthians 1:4,5-7; 2 Timothy 1:4-5.
17   1 Samuel 22:14.
18   1 Corinthians 13:6-7.
19   Psalm 15:3.
20   Proverbs 25:23.
21   Proverbs 26:24-25.
22   Psalm 101:5.
23   Proverbs 22:1; John 8:49.
24   Psalm 15:4.
25   Philippians 4:8.
26   1 Samuel 17:28; 2 Samuel 1:9,10,15-16; 16:3.
27   Leviticus 19:15; Habakkuk 1:4.
28   Proverbs 6:16,19; 19:5.
29   Acts 6:13.

wittingly appearing and pleading for an evil cause, defiance of and dominance over the truth;[1] passing unjust sentence,[2] calling evil good, and good evil; rewarding the wicked according to the work of the righteous, and the righteous according to the work of the wicked;[3] forgery,[4] concealing the truth, undue silence in a just cause,[5] and holding our peace when iniquity calls for either a reproof from us,[6] or complaint to others;[7] speaking the truth at a poor time,[8] or maliciously to a wrong end,[9] or perverting it to a wrong meaning,[10] or in doubtful and equivocal expression, to the prejudice of truth or justice;[11] speaking untruth,[12] lying,[13] slandering,[14] backbiting,[15] gossiping,[16] whispering,[17] scoffing,[18] using abusive language;[19] rash,[20] harsh,[21] and partial censuring;[22] misconstruing intentions, words, and actions;[23] flattering,[24] vain boasting,[25] thinking or speaking too highly or too poorly of ourselves or others;[26] denying the gifts and graces of God;[27] aggravating smaller faults;[28] hiding, excusing, or extenuating of sins, when called to a free confession;[29] unnecessary discovering of infirmities;[30] raising false rumors;[31] receiving and approving evil reports,[32] and stopping our ears against just defense;[33] evil suspicion;[34] envying or grieving at the deserved credit of

1   Psalm 12:3-4; 52:1-4; Jeremiah 9:3,5; Acts 24:2,5.
2   1 Kings 21:9-14; Proverbs 17:15.
3   Isaiah 5:23.
4   Psalm 119:69; Luke 16:5-7; 19:8.
5   Leviticus 5:1; Deuteronomy 13:8; Acts 5:3,8-9; 2 Timothy 4:6.
6   Leviticus 19:17; 1 Kings 1:6.
7   Isaiah 59:4.
8   Proverbs 29:11.
9   1 Samuel 22:9-10; Psalm 52:1-5.
10 Psalm 56:5; Matthew 26:60-61; John 2:19.
11 Genesis 3:5; 26:7,9.
12 Isaiah 59:13.
13 Leviticus 19:11.
14 Psalm 50:20.
15 Jeremiah 38:4; James 4:11.
16 Leviticus 19:19.
17 Romans 1:29-30.
18 Genesis 21:9; Galatians 4:29.
19 1 Corinthians 6:10.
20 Matthew 7:1.
21 Acts 28:4.
22 Genesis 38:24; Romans 2:1.
23 1 Samuel 1:13-15; 2 Samuel 10:3; Nehemiah 6:6-8; Psalm 69-10; Romans 3:8.
24 Psalm 12:2-3.
25 2 Timothy 3:2.
26 Exodus 4:10-14; Luke 18:9,11; Acts 12:22; Romans 12:16; 1 Corinthians 4:6.
27 Job 4:6; 27:5,6.
28 Matthew 7:3-5.
29 Genesis 3:12-13; 4:9; 2 Kings 5:25; Proverbs 28:13; Jeremiah 2:35.
30 Genesis 9:22; Proverbs 25:9-10.
31 Exodus 23:1.
32 Proverbs 29:12.
33 Job 31:13-14; Acts 7:56-57.
34 1 Corinthians 13:5; 1 Timothy 6:4.

anyone;[1] endeavoring or desiring to impair it,[2] rejoicing in the disgrace and bad reputation of anyone;[3] scornful contempt,[4] fond admiration,[5] breach of lawful promises;[6] neglecting such things as are of good report;[7] and practicing or not avoiding ourselves, or not hindering what we can in others, such things as result in an ill name.[8]

Q. 146. Which is the Tenth Commandment?

A. The Tenth Commandment is, "You shall not covet your neighbor's house; you shall not covet your neighbor's wife, or his male servant, or his female servant, or his ox, or his donkey, or anything that is your neighbor's."[9]

Q. 147. What are the duties required in the Tenth Commandment?

A. The duties required in the Tenth Commandment are: such a full contentment with our own condition,[10] and such a charitable frame of the whole soul toward our neighbor, so that all our inward motions and affections touching him, tend toward and further all the good that is his.[11]

Q. 148. What are the sins forbidden in the Tenth Commandment?

A. The sins forbidden in the Tenth Commandment are: discontent with our own estate;[12] envying,[13] and grieving at the good of our neighbor,[14] together with all inordinate motions and affections toward anything that is his.[15]

Q. 149. Is any man able perfectly to keep the commandments of God?

A. No man is able, either of himself,[16] or by any grace received in this life, perfectly to keep the commandments of God;[17] but does daily break them in thought,[18] word, and deed.[19]

---

1   Numbers 11:29; Matthew 21:15.
2   Ezra 4:12-13.
3   Jeremiah 48:27.
4   Psalm 35:15-16,21; Matthew 27:28-29.
5   Acts 12:22; Jude 16.
6   Romans 1:31; 2 Timothy 3:3.
7   1 Samuel 2:24.
8   2 Samuel 13:12-13; Proverbs 5:8-9; 6:33.
9   Exodus 20:17 (ESV).
10 1 Timothy 6:6; Hebrews 13:5.
11 Job 31:29; Esther 10:3; Psalm 122:7-9; Romans 12:15; 1 Corinthians 13:4-7; 1 Timothy 1:5.
12 1 Kings 21:4; Esther 5:13; 1 Corinthians 10:10.
13 Galatians 5:26; James 3:14,16.
14 Nehemiah 2:10; Psalm 112:9-10.
15 Deuteronomy 5:21; Romans 7:7-8; 13:9; Colossians 3:5.
16 John 15:5; Romans 8:3; James 3:2.
17 Ecclesiastes 7:20; Romans 7:18-19; Galatians 5:17; 1 John 1:8,10.
18 Genesis 6:5; 8:21.
19 Romans 3:9-19; James 3:2-13.

Q. 150. Are all transgressions of the law of God equally wicked in themselves, and in the sight of God?

A. All transgressions of the law of God are not equally wicked; but some sins in themselves, and by reason of aggravating circumstances, are more wicked in the sight of God than others.[1]

Q. 151. What are those aggravating circumstances that make some sins more wicked than others?

A. Sins receive their aggravated status,

1. From the persons offending:[2] if they be of more mature age,[3] greater experience of grace,[4] high regard for profession,[5] giftedness,[6] place,[7] office,[8] standing as guides to others,[9] and whose example is likely to be followed by others.[10]

2. From the parties offended:[11] if immediately against God,[12] His attributes,[13] and worship;[14] against Christ, and His grace:[15] the Holy Spirit,[16] His witness,[17] and workings;[18] against superiors, men of high standing,[19] and those to whom we stand especially related and engaged;[20] against any of the saints,[21] particularly weak brothers and sisters,[22] the souls of them or any other;[23] and the common good of all or many.[24]

3. From the nature and seriousness of the offense:[25] if it be against the express letter of the law,[26] break many commandments, contain in it many sins:[27] if not only conceived

1 Psalm 73:17,32,56; Ezekiel 8:6,13,15; John 19:11; 1 John 5:16.
2 Jeremiah 2:8.
3 Job 32:7,9; Ecclesiastes 4:13.
4 1 Kings 11:4,9.
5 2 Samuel 12:14; 1 Corinthians 5:1.
6 Luke 12:47-48; James 4:17.
7 Jeremiah 5:4-5.
8 2 Samuel 12:7-9; Ezekiel 8:11-12.
9 Romans 2:17-24.
10 Galatians 2:11-14.
11 Matthew 21:38-39.
12 1 Samuel 2:25; Psalm 5:4; Acts 5:4.
13 Romans 2:4.
14 Malachi 1:8,14.
15 Hebrews 2:2-3; 7:25.
16 Matthew 12:31-32; Hebrews 10:29.
17 Ephesians 4:30.
18 Hebrews 6:4-6.
19 Numbers 12:8-9; Isaiah 3:5; Jude 8.
20 Psalm 55:12-15; Proverbs 30:17; 2 Corinthians 12:15.
21 Zephaniah 2:8,10-11; Matthew 18:6; 1 Corinthians 6:8; Revelation 17:6.
22 Romans 14:13,15,21; 1 Corinthians 8:11-12.
23 Ezekiel 13:19; Matthew 23:15; 1 Corinthians 8:12;
24 Joshua 22:20; 1 Thessalonians 2:15-16.
25 Proverbs 6:30-33.
26 1 Kings 11:9-10; Ezra 9:10-12.
27 Joshua 7:21; Proverbs 5:8-12; 6:32-33; Colossians 3:5; 1 Timothy 6:10.

in the heart, but carried out in words and actions,[1] scandalize others,[2] and permit no compensation:[3] if against means,[4] mercies,[5] judgments,[6] light of nature,[7] conviction of conscience,[8] public or private admonition,[9] censures of the church,[10] civil punishments;[11] and our prayers, purposes, promises,[12] vows,[13] covenants,[14] and engagements to God or men:[15] if done deliberately,[16] willfully,[17] presumptuously,[18] impudently,[19] boastingly,[20] maliciously,[21] frequently,[22] obstinately,[23] with light,[24] repeatedly,[25] or relapsing after repentance.[26]

4. From circumstances of time,[27] and place:[28] if on the Lord's Day,[29] or other times of divine worship;[30] or immediately before,[31] or after these,[32] or other situations that should prevent or remedy such miscarriages;[33] if in public, or in the presence of others, who are thereby likely to be provoked or corrupted.[34]

Q. 152. What does every sin deserve at the hands of God?

A.   Every sin, even the least, being against the sovereignty,[35] goodness,[36] and holiness of God,[37] and against His righteous law,[38] deserves His wrath and curse,[39] both in this life,[40] and that which is to come;[41] and cannot be expiated but by the blood of Christ.[42]

1   Micah 2:1; Matthew 5:22; James 1:14-15.
2   Matthew 18:7; Romans 2:23-24.
3   Deuteronomy 22:22,28-29; Proverbs 7:32-35.
4   Matthew 11:21-24; John 15:22.
5   Deuteronomy 32:6; Isaiah 1:3.
6   Jeremiah 5:3; Amos 4:8-11.
7   Romans 1:26-27.
8   Daniel 5:22; Romans 1:32; Titus 3:10-11.
9   Proverbs 29:1.
10   Matthew 18:17; Titus 3:10.
11   Proverbs 23:35; 27:22.
12   Psalm 73:34-37; Jeremiah 2:20; 45:5-6,20-21.
13   Proverbs 20:25; Ecclesiastes 5:4-6.
14   Leviticus 26:25.
15   Proverbs 2:17; Ezekiel 7:18-19.
16   Psalm 36:4.
17   Jeremiah 6:16.
18   Exodus 21:14; Numbers 15:30.
19   Proverbs 7:13; Jeremiah 3:3.
20   Psalm 52:1.
21   3 John 10.
22   Numbers 15:22.
23   Zechariah 7:11-12.
24   Proverbs 2:14.
25   Isaiah 57:17.
26   Jeremiah 34:8-11; 2 Peter 2:20-22.
27   2 Kings 5:26.
28   Isaiah 26:10; Jeremiah 7:10.
29   Ezekiel 23:37-39.
30   Numbers 25:6-7; Isaiah 58:3-5.
31   1 Corinthians 11:20-21.
32   Proverbs 7:14-15; Jeremiah 7:8-10; John 13:27,30.
33   Ezra 9:13-14.
34   1 Samuel 2:22-24; 2 Samuel 16:22.
35   James 2:10-11.
36   Exodus 20:1-2.
37   Leviticus 10:3; 11:44-45; Habakkuk 1:13.
38   Romans 7:12; 1 John 3:4.
39   Galatians 3:10; Ephesians 5:6.
40   Deuteronomy 20:15-20; Lamentations 3:39.
41   Matthew 25:41.
42   Hebrews 9:22; 1 Peter 1:18-19.

Q. 153. What does God require of us, that we may escape His wrath and curse due to us by reason of the transgression of the law?

A. That we may escape the wrath and curse of God due to us by reason of the transgression of the law, He requires of us repentance toward God, and faith toward our Lord Jesus Christ,[1] and the diligent use of the outward means by which Christ communicates to us the benefits of His mediation.[2]

Q. 154. What are the outward means by which Christ communicates to us the benefits of His mediation?

A. The outward and ordinary means, by which Christ communicates to His church the benefits of His mediation, are all His ordinances, especially the Word, sacraments, and prayer, all of which are made effectual to the elect for their salvation.[3]

Q. 155. How is the Word made effectual to salvation?

A. The Spirit of God makes the reading, but especially the preaching of the Word, an effectual means of enlightening,[4] convincing, and humbling sinners,[5] of driving them out of themselves, and drawing them to Christ,[6] of conforming them to His image,[7] and subduing them to His will;[8] of strengthening them against temptations and corruptions;[9] of building them up in grace,[10] and establishing their hearts in holiness and comfort through faith to salvation.[11]

Q. 156. Is the Word of God to be read by all?

A. Although all are not permitted to read the Word publicly to the congregation,[12] yet all sorts of people are bound to read it apart by themselves,[13] and with their families;[14] to which end, the Holy Scriptures are to be translated out of the original into the language of every people to whom they come.[15]

---

1 Matthew 3:7-8; Luke 13:3,5; John 3:16,18; Acts 16:30-31; 20:21.
2 Proverbs 2:1-5; 8:33-36.
3 Matthew 28:19-20; Acts 2:42,46-47.
4 Nehemiah 8:8; Psalm 19:8; Acts 26:18.
5 1 Chronicles 14:24-25; 2 Chronicles 34:18,19,26-28.
6 Acts 2:37,41; 8:27-30,35-38.
7 2 Corinthians 3:18.
8 Romans 6:17; 2 Corinthians 10:4-6.
9 Psalm 19:11; Matthew 4:4,7,10; 1 Corinthians 10:11; Ephesians 6:16-17.
10 Acts 20:32; 2 Timothy 3:15-17.
11 Romans 1:16; 10:13-17; 15:4; 16:25; 1 Thessalonians 3:2,10-11,13.
12 Deuteronomy 31:9,11-13; Nehemiah 8:2-3; 9:3-5.
13 Deuteronomy 17:19; Isaiah 34:16; John 5:39; Revelation 1:8.
14 Genesis 18:17,19; Deuteronomy 6:6-9; Psalm 78:5-7.
15 1 Corinthians 14:6,9,11-12,15-16,24,27-28.

Q. 157. How is the Word of God to be read?

A.   The Holy Scriptures are to be read with a high and reverent esteem of them;[1] with a firm conviction that they are the very Word of God,[2] and that only He can enable us to understand them;[3] with desire to know, believe, and obey, the will of God revealed in them;[4] with diligence,[5] and attention to the matter and scope of them;[6] with meditation,[7] application,[8] self-denial,[9] and prayer.[10]

Q. 158. By whom is the Word of God to be preached?

A.   The Word of God is to be preached only by such as are sufficiently gifted,[11] and also duly approved and called to that office.[12]

Q. 159. How is the Word of God to be preached by those who are called to do so?

A.   They who are called to labor in the ministry of the Word are to preach sound doctrine,[13] diligently,[14] in season, and out of season;[15] plainly,[16] not in the enticing words of man's wisdom, but in demonstration of the Spirit, and of power;[17] faithfully,[18] making known the whole counsel of God;[19] wisely,[20] applying themselves to the needs and abilities of the hearers;[21] zealously,[22] with fervent love to God,[23] and the souls of His people;[24] sincerely,[25] aiming at His glory,[26] and their conversion,[27] edification,[28] and salvation.[29]

---

1 Exodus 24:7; 2 Chronicles 34:27; Nehemiah 8:3-6,10; Psalm 19:10; Isaiah 66:2; 2
2 2 Peter 1:19-21.
3 Luke 24:45; 2 Corinthians 3:13-16.
4 Deuteronomy 17:10,20.
5 Acts 17:11.
6 Luke 10:26-28; Acts 8:30,34.
7 Psalm 1:2; 119:97.
8 2 Chronicles 34:21.
9 Deuteronomy 33:3; Proverbs 3:5.
10 Nehemiah 7:6,8; Psalm 119:18; Proverbs 2:1-6.
11 Hosea 4:6; Malachi 2:7; 2 Corinthians 3:6; Ephesians 4:8-11; 1 Timothy 3:2,6.
12 Jeremiah 14:15; Romans 10:15; 1 Corinthians 12:28-29; 1 Timothy 3:10; 5:22; 9:14; Hebrews 5:4.

13 Titus 2:1,8.
14 Acts 18:25.
15 2 Timothy 4:2.
16 1 Corinthians 14:19.
17 1 Corinthians 2:4.
18 Jeremiah 23:28; 1 Corinthians 4:1-2.
19 Acts 20:27.
20 Colossians 1:28; 2 Timothy 2:15.
21 Luke 12:42; 1 Corinthians 3:2; Hebrews 5:12-14.
22 Acts 18:25.
23 2 Corinthians 5:13-14; Philippians 1:15-17.
24 2 Corinthians 12:15; Colossians 4:12.
25 2 Corinthians 2:17; 4:2.
26 John 7:18; 1 Thessalonians 2:4-6.
27 1 Corinthians 9:19-22.
28 2 Corinthians 12:19; Ephesians 4:12.
29 Acts 26:16-18; 1 Timothy 4:16.

Q. 160. What is required of those who hear the Word preached?

A.   It is required of those who hear the Word preached, that they attend to it with diligence,[1] preparation,[2] and prayer;[3] examine what they hear by the Scriptures;[4] receive the truth with faith,[5] love,[6] meekness,[7] and readiness of mind,[8] as the Word of God;[9] meditate,[10] and discuss it;[11] hide it in their hearts,[12] and bring forth the fruit of it in their lives.[13]

Q. 161. How do the sacraments become effectual means of salvation?

A.   The sacraments become effectual means of salvation, not by any power in them or any virtue derived from the piety or intention of him by whom they are administered; but only by the working of the Holy Spirit, and the blessing of Christ by whom they are instituted.[14]

Q. 162. What is a sacrament?

A.   A sacrament is a holy ordinance instituted by Christ in His church,[15] to signify, seal and exhibit[16] to those who are within the Covenant of Grace,[17] the benefits of His mediation;[18] to strengthen and increase their faith and all other graces;[19] to oblige them to obedience;[20] to testify and cherish their love and communion with one another,[21] and to distinguish them from those who are outside the Covenant of Grace.[22]

Q. 163. What are the parts of a sacrament?

A.   The parts of a sacrament are two: the one, an outward and perceptible sign used according to Christ's own direction; the other, an inward and spiritual grace signified by it.[23]

1   Proverbs 8:34.
2   Luke 8:18; 1 Peter 2:1-2.
3   Psalm 119:18; Ephesians 6:18-19.
4   Acts 17:11.
5   Hebrews 4:2.
6   2 Thessalonians 2:10.
7   James 1:21.
8   Acts 17:11.
9   1 Thessalonians 2:13.
10 Luke 9:44; Hebrews 2:1.
11 Deuteronomy 6:6-7; Luke 24:14.
12 Psalm 119:11; Proverbs 2:1.
13 Luke 8:15; James 1:25.
14 Acts 8:13,23; 1 Corinthians 3:6-7; 12:13; 1 Peter 3:21.
15 Genesis 17:7,10; Exodus 12; Matthew 26:26-28; 28:19.
16 Romans 4:11; 1 Corinthians 11:24-25.
17 Exodus 12:48; Romans 15:8.
18 Acts 2:38; 1 Corinthians 10:16.
19 Romans 4:11; Galatians 3:27.
20 Romans 6:3-4; 1 Corinthians 10:21.
21 1 Corinthians 12:13; Ephesians 4:2-5.
22 Genesis 34:14; Ephesians 2:11-12.
23 Matthew 3:11; Romans 2:28-29; 1 Peter 3:21.

Q. 164. How many sacraments has Christ instituted under the New Testament?

A.   Under the New Testament, Christ has instituted in His church only two sacraments, Baptism, and the Lord's Supper.[1]

Q. 165. What is Baptism?

A.   Baptism is a sacrament of the New Testament, in which Christ has ordained the washing with water in the name of the Father, and of the Son, and of the Holy Spirit,[2] to be a sign and seal of ingrafting to Himself,[3] of remission of sins by His blood,[4] and regeneration by His Spirit;[5] of adoption,[6] and resurrection to everlasting life:[7] and by which the parties baptized are solemnly admitted into the visible church,[8] and enter an open and professed engagement to be wholly and only the Lord's.[9]

Q. 166. To whom is Baptism to be administered?

A.   Baptism is not to be administered to any who are out of the visible church, and so strangers from the Covenant of Promise, till they profess their faith in Christ, and obedience to Him;[10] but infants descending from parents, either both or but one of them, professing faith in Christ, and obedience to Him, are, in that respect, within the covenant, and are to be baptized.[11]

Q. 167. How is our Baptism to be improved by us?

A.   The needful but much neglected duty of improving our Baptism, is to be performed by us all of our lives, especially in the time of temptation, and when we are present at the administration of it to others,[12] by serious and thankful consideration of the nature of it and of the ends for which Christ instituted it, the privileges and benefits conferred and sealed by it, and our

---

1   Matthew 26:26,27,28; 28:19; 1 Corinthians 11:20,23.
2   Matthew 28:19.
3   Galatians 3:27.
4   Mark 1:4; Revelation 1:5.
5   Ephesians 5:26; Titus 3:5.
6   Galatians 3:26-27.
7   Romans 6:5; 1 Corinthians 15:29.

8   1 Corinthians 12:13.
9   Romans 6:4.
10   Acts 2:38; 8:36-37.
11   Genesis 17:7,9; Matthew 28:19; Luke 18:15-16; Acts 2:38-39; Romans 4:11-12; 11:16; 1 Corinthians 7:14; Galatians 3:9; Colossians 2:11-12.
12   Romans 6:4,6,11; Colossians 2:11-12.

solemn vow made in it;[1] by being humbled for our sinful corruption, our falling short of, and walking contrary to, the grace of Baptism and our engagements;[2] by growing up to assurance of pardon of sin, and of all other blessings sealed to us in that sacrament;[3] by drawing strength from the death and resurrection of Christ, into whom we are baptized, for the dying to sin, and being made alive in grace;[4] and by endeavoring to live by faith,[5] to have our conversation in holiness and righteousness,[6] as those who have thus given up their names to Christ,[7] and to walk in brotherly love, as being baptized by the same Spirit into one body.[8]

Q. 168. What is the Lord's Supper?

A. The Lord's Supper is a sacrament of the New Testament,[9] in which by giving and receiving bread and wine according to the direction of Jesus Christ, His death is shown forth; and they that worthily communicate, feed upon His body and blood to their spiritual nourishment and growth in grace;[10] have their union and communion with Him confirmed;[11] testify and renew their thankfulness[12] and engagement to God,[13] and their mutual love and fellowship with each other, as members of the same mystical body.[14]

Q. 169. How has Christ appointed bread and wine to be given and received in the sacrament of the Lord's Supper?

A. Christ has appointed the ministers of His Word in the administration of this sacrament of the Lord's Supper, to set apart the bread and wine from common use by the words of institution, thanksgiving, and prayer; to take and break the bread, and to give both the bread and the wine to the communicants; who

1   Romans 6:3-5.
2   Romans 6:2-3; 1 Corinthians 1:11-13.
3   Romans 4:11-12; 1 Peter 3:21.
4   Romans 6:3,4,5.
5   Galatians 3:26-27.
6   Romans 6:22.
7   Acts 2:38.
8   1 Corinthians 12:13,25.
9   Luke 22:20.
10 Matthew 26:26-28; 1 Corinthians 11:23-26.
11 1 Corinthians 10:16.
12 1 Corinthians 11:24.
13 1 Corinthians 10:14-16,21.
14 1 Corinthians 10:17.

are by the same direction to take and eat the bread, and to drink the wine; in thankful remembrance that the body of Christ was broken and given, and His blood shed for them.[1]

Q. 170. How do they who worthily communicate in the Lord's Supper feed upon the body and blood of Christ in it?

A. As the body and the blood of Christ are not corporally or carnally present in, with, or under the bread and wine in the Lord's Supper;[2] and yet are spiritually present to the faith of the receiver, no less truly and really than the elements themselves are to their outward senses;[3] so they who worthily communicate in the sacrament of the Lord's Supper, do in it feed upon the body and blood of Christ, not after a corporal or carnal, but in a spiritual manner; yet truly and really,[4] while by faith they receive and apply to themselves Christ crucified, and all the benefits of His death.[5]

Q. 171. How are they who receive the sacrament of the Lord's Supper to prepare themselves before they come to it?

A. They who receive the sacrament of the Lord's Supper are, before they come, to prepare themselves for it; by examining themselves,[6] of their being in Christ,[7] of their sins and wants;[8] of the truth and measure of their knowledge,[9] faith,[10] repentance,[11] love to God and the brothers,[12] charity to all men,[13] forgiving those who have done them wrong;[14] of their desires after Christ,[15] and of their new obedience;[16] and by renewing the exercise of these graces,[17] by serious meditation,[18] and fervent prayer.[19]

---

1 Matthew 26:26-28; Mark 14:22-24;
   Luke 22:19-20; 1 Corinthians 11:23-24.
2 Acts 3:21.
3 Matthew 26:26,28.
4 1 Corinthians 11:24-29.
5 1 Corinthians 10:16.
6 1 Corinthians 11:28.
7 Corinthians 13:5.
8 Exodus 12:15; 1 Corinthians 5:7.
9 1 Corinthians 11:29.
10 Matthew 26:28; 1 Corinthians 13:5.
11 Zechariah 12:10; 1 Corinthians 11:31.
12 Acts 2:46-47; 1 Corinthians 10:16-17.
13 1 Corinthians 5:8; 11:18,20.
14 Matthew 5:23-24.
15 Isaiah 55:1; John 7:37.
16 1 Corinthians 5:7-8.
17 Psalm 26:6; 1 Corinthians 11:25-26,28;
    Hebrews 10:21-22,24.
18 1 Corinthians 11:24-25.
19 2 Chronicles 30:18-19; Matthew 26:26.

Q. 172. May one who doubts of his being in Christ, or of his due preparation, come to the Lord's Supper?

A. One who doubts of his being in Christ, or of his due preparation for the sacrament of the Lord's Supper, may have true interest in Christ, though he is not yet assured of it;[1] and in God's
account has it, if he is duly affected with the fear of the want of
it,[2] and truly desires to be found in Christ,[3] and to depart from
iniquity;[4] in which case (because promises are made, and this
sacrament is appointed, for the relief even of weak and doubt-
ing Christians)[5] he is to grieve his unbelief,[6] and labor to have
his doubts resolved;[7] and so doing, he may and ought to come
to the Lord's Supper, that he may be further strengthened.[8]

Q. 173. May any who profess the faith, and desire to come to the Lord's
Supper, be kept from it?

A. Those who are found to be ignorant or scandalous, notwithstanding their profession of the faith, and desire to come to the
Lord's Supper, may and ought to be kept from that sacrament
by the power that Christ has left in His church,[9] until they
receive instruction, and demonstrate their reformation.[10]

Q. 174. What is required of those who receive the sacrament of the
Lord's Supper in the time of the administration of it?

A. It is required of those who receive the sacrament of the Lord's
Supper that, during the time of the administration of it, with all
holy reverence and attention, they wait upon God in that ordinance;[11] diligently observe the sacramental elements and

---

1 Psalm 77:1-4,7-10; Psalm 88; Isaiah 50:10; Jonah 2:4; 1 John 5:13.
2 Psalm 31:22; 73:13,22-23; Isaiah 54:7-10; Matthew 5:3-4.
3 Psalm 10:17; 42:1-2,5; Philippians 3:8-9.
4 Psalm 66:18-20; Isaiah 50:10; 2 Timothy 2:19.
5 Isaiah 40:11,29,31; Matthew 11:28; 12:20; 26:28.
6 Mark 9:24.
7 Acts 2:37; 16:30.
8 Romans 4:11; 1 Corinthians 11:28.
9 Matthew 7:6; 1 Corinthians 5 to the end; 11:27-31; 1 Timothy 5:22.
10 2 Corinthians 2:7.
11 Leviticus 10:3; Psalm 5:7; 1 Corinthians 11:17,26-27; Hebrews 12:28.

actions;[1] heedfully discern the Lord's body,[2] and affectionately meditate on His death and sufferings,[3] and thereby stir up themselves to a vigorous exercise of their graces;[4] in judging themselves,[5] and sorrowing for sin;[6] in earnest hungering and thirsting after Christ,[7] feeding on Him by faith,[8] receiving of His fullness,[9] trusting in His merits,[10] rejoicing in His love,[11] giving thanks for His grace;[12] in renewing of their covenant with God,[13] and love to all the saints.[14]

Q. 175. What is the duty of Christians after they have received the sacrament of the Lord's Supper?

A. The duty of Christians after they have received the sacrament of the Lord's Supper, is seriously to consider how they have behaved themselves in it, and with what success;[15] if they find quickening and comfort, to bless God for it,[16] beg the continuance of it,[17] watch against relapse,[18] fulfill their vows,[19] and encourage themselves to a frequent attendance on that ordinance:[20] but if they find no present benefit, more exactly to review their preparation for, and posture at, the sacrament;[21] in both which if they can approve themselves to God and their own consciences, they are to wait for the fruit of it in due time;[22] but if they see that they have failed in either, they are to be humbled,[23] and to attend upon it afterward with more care and diligence.[24]

1   Exodus 24:8; Matthew 26:28.
2   1 Corinthians 11:29.
3   Luke 22:19.
4   1 Corinthians 10:3-5,11,14; 11:26.
5   1 Corinthians 11:31.
6   Zechariah 12:20.
7   Revelation 22:17.
8   John 6:35.
9   John 1:16.
10 Philippians 1:16.
11 2 Chronicles 30:21; Psalm 58:4-5.
12 Psalm 22:26.
13 Psalm 50:5; Jeremiah 50:5.
14 Acts 2:42.
15 Psalm 28:7; 85:8; 1 Corinthians 11:7,30-31.
16 2 Chronicles 30:21-23,25-26; Acts 2:42,46-47.
17 1 Chronicles 29:18; Psalm 36:10; Song of Solomon 3:4.
18 1 Corinthians 10:3-5,12.
19 Psalm 50:14.
20 Acts 2:42,46; 1 Corinthians 11:25-26.
21 Ecclesiastes 5:1-6; Song of Solomon 5:1-6.
22 Psalm 42:5,8; 43:3-5; 123:1-2.
23 2 Chronicles 30:18-19.
24 1 Chronicles 15:12-14; 2 Corinthians 7:11.

Q. 176. In what do the sacraments of Baptism and the Lord's Supper agree?

A. The sacraments of Baptism and the Lord's Supper agree, in that the Author of both is God;[1] the spiritual part of both is Christ and His benefits;[2] both are seals of the same covenant,[3] are to be dispensed by ministers of the Gospel and by none other,[4] and to be continued in the church of Christ until his second coming.[5]

Q. 177. In what do the sacraments of Baptism and the Lord's Supper differ?

A. The sacraments of Baptism and the Lord's Supper differ in that Baptism is to be administered but once, with water, to be a sign and seal of our regeneration and ingrafting to Christ,[6] and that even to infants;[7] whereas the Lord's Supper is to be administered often, in the elements of bread and wine, to represent and exhibit Christ as spiritual nourishment to the soul,[8] and to confirm our continuance and growth in Him,[9] and that only to those who are of years and ability to examine themselves.[10]

Q. 178. What is prayer?

A. Prayer is an offering up of our desires to God,[11] in the name of Christ,[12] by the help of His Spirit,[13] with confession of our sins,[14] and thankful acknowledgment of his mercies.[15]

Q. 179. Are we to pray to God only?

A. God only being able to search the heart,[16] hear the requests,[17] pardon the sins,[18] and fulfill the desires of all,[19] and only to be

1   Matthew 28:19; 1 Corinthians 11:23.
2   Romans 6:3-4; 1 Corinthians 10:16.
3   Matthew 26:27-28; Romans 4:11; Colossians 2:12.
4   Matthew 28:19; John 1:33; 1 Corinthians 4:1; 11:23; Hebrews 5:4.
5   Matthew 28:19-20; 1 Corinthians 11:26.
6   Matthew 3:11; Galatians 3:27; Titus 3:5.
7   Genesis 17:7,9; Acts 2:38-39; 1 Corinthians 7:14.
8   1 Corinthians 11:23-26.
9   1 Corinthians 10:16.
10 1 Corinthians 11:28-29.
11 Psalm 57:8.
12 John 16:23.
13 Romans 8:26.
14 Psalm 32:5-6; Daniel 9:4.
15 Philippians 4:6.
16 1 Kings 8:39; Acts 1:24; Romans 8:27.
17 Psalm 65:2.
18 Micah 7:18.
19 Psalm 145:18.

believed in,[1] and worshiped with religious worship;[2] prayer, which is a special part of it,[3] is to be made by all to Him alone,[4] and to none other.[5]

Q. 180. What is it to pray in the name of Christ?

A.   To pray in the name of Christ is, in obedience to His command, and with confidence in His promises, to ask mercy for His sake:[6] not by bare mentioning of His name;[7] but by drawing our encouragement to pray, and our boldness, strength, and hope of acceptance in prayer, from Christ and His mediation.[8]

Q. 181. Why are we to pray in the name of Christ?

A.   The sinfulness of man, and his distance from God by reason of it, being so great, as that we can have no access into His presence without a mediator,[9] and there being none in heaven or earth appointed to, or fit for, that glorious work but Christ alone,[10] we are to pray in no other name but His only.[11]

Q. 182. How does the Spirit help us to pray?

A.   Because we do not know for what to pray as we ought, the Spirit helps our weaknesses, by enabling us to understand both for whom, and what, and how prayer is to be made; and by working and making alive in our hearts (although not in all persons, nor at all times in the same measure) those understandings, affections, and graces that are necessary for the right performance of that duty.[12]

---

1   Romans 10:14.
2   Matthew 4:10.
3   1 Corinthians 1:2.
4   Psalm 50:15.
5   Romans 10:14.
6   Daniel 9:17; John 14:13-14; 16:24.

7   Matthew 7:21.
8   Hebrews 4:14-16; 1 John 5:13-15.
9   Isaiah 59:2; John 14:6; Ephesians 3:12.
10 John 6:27; 1 Timothy 2:5; Hebrews 7:25-27.
11 Colossians 3:17; Hebrews 13:15.
12 Psalm 10:17; Zechariah 12:10; Romans 8:26-27.

Q. 183. For whom are we to pray?

A. We are to pray for the whole church of Christ on earth,[1] for
government officials,[2] and ministers,[3] for ourselves,[4] our brothers and sisters,[5] even our enemies,[6] and for all sorts of men living,[7] or who shall live hereafter;[8] but not for the dead.[9]

Q. 184. For what things are we to pray?

A. We are to pray for all things tending to the glory of God,[10] the
welfare of the church,[11] our own[12] or others' good;[13] but not
for anything that is unlawful.[14]

Q. 185. How are we to pray?

A. We are to pray with an awe-inspiring understanding of the
majesty of God,[15] and deep sense of our own unworthiness,[16]
needs,[17] and sins;[18] with repentant,[19] thankful,[20] and open
hearts;[21] with understanding,[22] faith,[23] sincerity,[24] emotion,[25]
love,[26] and perseverance,[27] waiting for Him[28] with humble
submission to His will.[29]

Q. 186. What rule has God given for our direction in the duty of prayer?

A. The whole Word of God is of use to direct us in the duty of
praying;[30] but the special rule of direction is that form of prayer
that our Savior Christ taught His disciples, commonly called,
"the Lord's Prayer."[31]

Q. 187. How is the Lord's Prayer to be used?

A. The Lord's Prayer is not only for direction, as a pattern according to which we are to make other prayers; but may be also
used itself as a prayer so that it is done with understanding,

1   Psalm 28:9; Ephesians 6:18.
2   1 Timothy 2:1-2.
3   Colossians 4:3.
4   Genesis 32:11.
5   James 5:16.
6   Matthew 5:44.
7   1 Timothy 2:1-2.
8   2 Samuel 7:29; John 17:20.
9   2 Samuel 12:21-23.
10 Matthew 6:9.
11 Psalm 51:18; 122:6.
12 Matthew 7:11.
13 Psalm 125:4.
14 1 John 5:14.
15 Ecclesiastes 5:1.
16 Genesis 18:27; 32:10.
17 Luke 15:17-19.
18 Luke 18:13-14.
19 Psalm 51:17.
20 Philippians 4:6.
21 1 Samuel 1:15; 2:1.
22 1 Corinthians 14:15.
23 Mark 11:24; James 1:6.
24 Psalm 17:1; 145:18.
25 James 5:16.
26 1 Timothy 2:8.
27 Ephesians 6:18.
28 Micah 7:7.
29 Matthew 26:39.
30 1 John 5:14.
31 Matthew 6:9-13; Luke 11:2-4.

faith, reverence, and other graces necessary to the right performance of the duty of prayer.[1]

Q. 188. Of how many parts does the Lord's Prayer consist?

A. The Lord's Prayer consists of three parts: a preface, petitions, and a conclusion.

Q. 189. What does the preface of the Lord's Prayer teach us?

A. The preface of the Lord's Prayer (contained in the words, "Our Father in heaven")[2] teaches us, when we pray, to draw near to God with confidence of His fatherly goodness, and our interest in it;[3] with reverence, and all other childlike attitudes,[4] heavenly affections,[5] and due understanding of His sovereign power, majesty, and gracious condescension:[6] as also to pray with and for others.[7]

Q. 190. For what do we pray in the first petition?

A. In the first petition (which is, "Hallowed be your name"[8]), acknowledging the utter inability and unwillingness in ourselves and all men to honor God rightly,[9] we pray: that God would by his grace enable and make us and others willing to know, to acknowledge, and highly esteem Him,[10] His titles,[11] attributes,[12] ordinances, Word,[13] works, and whatever He is pleased to make Himself known by;[14] and to glorify Him in thought, word,[15] and deed;[16] that He would prevent and remove atheism,[17] ignorance,[18] idolatry,[19] profaneness,[20] and whatever is dishonoring to Him;[21] and by His overruling providence, direct and arrange all things to His own glory.[22]

1   Matthew 6:9; Luke 11:2.
2   Matthew 6:9.
3   Luke 11:13; Romans 8:15.
4   Isaiah 64:9.
5   Psalm 123:1; Lamentations 3:41.
6   Nehemiah 1:4-6; Isaiah 63:15-16.
7   Acts 12:5.
8   Matthew 6:9.
9   Psalm 51:15; 2 Corinthians 3:5.
10 Psalm 67:2-3.
11 Psalm 83:18.
12 Psalm 86:10-13,15.
13 Psalm 138:1-3; 147:19-20; 2 Corinthians 2:14-15; 2 Thessalonians 3:1.
14 Psalm 8; 145.
15 Psalm 19:14; 103:1.
16 Philippians 1:9,11.
17 Psalm 67:1-4.
18 Ephesians 1:17-18.
19 Psalm 97:7.
20 Psalm 74:18,22-23.
21 2 Kings 19:15-16.
22 2 Chronicles 20:6,10-12; Psalm 83; 140:4,8.

Q. 191. For what do we pray in the second petition?

A. In the second petition (which is, "Your kingdom come"[1]),
acknowledging ourselves and all mankind to be by nature
under the dominion of sin and Satan,[2] we pray: that the kingdom of sin and Satan may be destroyed,[3] the Gospel spread
throughout the world,[4] the Jews called,[5] the fullness of the
Gentiles brought in;[6] that the church may be furnished with all
Gospel officers and ordinances,[6] purged from corruption,[7]
approved and maintained by the civil magistrate;[8] that the ordinances of Christ may be purely dispensed, and made effectual
to the converting of those who are yet in their sins, and the
confirming, comforting, and building up of those who are
already converted;[9] that Christ would rule in our hearts here,[11]
and hasten the time of His second coming, and our reigning
with Him forever;[12] and that He would be pleased so to exercise the kingdom of His power in all the world, as may best
bring about these ends.[13]

Q. 192. For what do we pray in the third petition?

A. In the third petition (which is, "Your will be done, on earth as it
is in heaven"[14]), acknowledging that by nature we and all men
are not only utterly unable and unwilling to know and do the
will of God,[15] but prone to rebel against His Word,[16] to com-
plain and murmur against his providence,[17] and wholly
inclined to do the will of the flesh, and of the devil:[18] we pray
that God would by His Spirit take away from us and others all
blindness,[19] weakness,[20] unwillingness,[21] and perverseness of

1   Matthew 6:10.
2   Ephesians 2:2-3.
3   Psalm 67:1,18; Revelation 12:10-11.
4   2 Thessalonians 3:1.
5   Romans 10:1.
6   Psalm 67; John 17:9,20; Romans 11:25-26.
7   Matthew 9:38; 2 Thessalonians 3:1.
8   Zephaniah 3:9; Malachi 1:11.
9   1 Timothy 2:1-2.
10 Acts 4:29-30; Romans 15:29-30,32; Ephesians
    6:18-20; 2 Thessalonians 1:11; 2:16-17.
11 Ephesians 3:14-20.
12 Revelation 22:20.
13 Isaiah 64:1-2; Revelation 4:8-11.
14 Matthew 6:10.
15 Job 21:14; Romans 7:18; 1 Corinthians 2:14.
16 Romans 8:7.
17 Exodus 17:7; Numbers 14:2.
18 Ephesians 2:2.
19 Ephesians 1:17-18.
20 Ephesians 3:16.
21 Matthew 26:40-41.

heart,[1] and by His grace make us able and willing to know, do, and submit to His will in all things,[2] with the like humility,[3] cheerfulness,[4] faithfulness,[5] diligence,[6] zeal,[7] sincerity,[8] and faithfulness,[9] as the angels do in heaven.[10]

Q. 193. For what do we pray in the fourth petition?

A.   In the fourth petition (which is, "Give us this day our daily bread"[11]), acknowledging that in Adam, and by our own sin, we have forfeited our right to all the outward blessings of this life, and deserve to be wholly deprived of them by God, and to have them cursed to us in the use of them;[12] and that these outward blessings alone are unable to sustain us,[13] nor can we merit them,[14] or by our own work obtain them,[15] but we are prone to desire,[16] get,[17] and use them unlawfully:[18] we pray for ourselves and others, that both they and we, waiting on the providence of God from day to day in the use of lawful means may, of his free gift, and as to his fatherly wisdom shall seem best, enjoy a sufficient portion of them,[19] and have the same continued and blessed to us in our holy and comfortable use of them,[20] and contentment in them;[21] and be kept from all things that are contrary to our material support and comfort.[22]

1	Jeremiah 31:18-19.	13	Deuteronomy 8:3.
2	Psalm 119:1,8,35-36; Acts 21:14.	14	Genesis 32:10.
3	Micah 6:8.	15	Deuteronomy 8:17-18.
4	2 Samuel 15:25-26; Job 1:21; Psalm 100:2.	16	Jeremiah 6:13; Mark 7:21-22.
5	Isaiah 38:3.	17	Hosea 12:7.
6	Psalm 119:4-5.	18	James 4:3.
7	Romans 12:11.	19	Genesis 28:20; 43:12-14; Ephesians 4:28;
8	Psalm 119:80.		Philippians 4:6; 2 Thessalonians 3:11-12.
9	Psalm 119:112.	20	1 Timothy 4:3-5.
10	Isaiah 6:2-3; Matthew 18:10.	21	1 Timothy 6:6-8.
11	Matthew 6:11.	22	Proverbs 30:8-9.
12	Genesis 2:17; 3:17; Deuteronomy 28:15-17; Jeremiah 5:25; Romans 8:20-22.		

Q. 194. For what do we pray for in the fifth petition?

A. In the fifth petition (which is, "Forgive us our debts, as we also have forgiven our debtors"[1]), acknowledging that we and all others are guilty both of original and actual sin, and thereby become debtors to the justice of God, and neither we nor any other creature can make the least satisfaction for that debt:[2] we pray for ourselves and others, that God of his free grace would, through the obedience and satisfaction of Christ understood and applied by faith, acquit us both from the guilt and punishment of sin,[3] accept us in His Beloved,[4] continue His favor and grace to us,[5] pardon our daily failings,[6] and fill us with peace and joy, in giving us daily more and more assurance of forgiveness;[7] which we are more emboldened to ask, and encouraged to expect, when we have this testimony in ourselves, that we from the heart forgive others their offenses.[8]

Q. 195. For what do we pray in the sixth petition?

A. In the sixth petition (which is, "And lead us not into temptation, but deliver us from evil"[9]), acknowledging that the most wise, righteous, and gracious God, for various holy and just ends, may so order things that we may be assaulted, foiled, and for a time led captive by temptations;[10] that Satan,[11] the world,[12] and the flesh, are ready powerfully to draw us aside and ensnare us;[13] and that we, even after the pardon of our sins, by reason of our corruption,[14] weakness, and lack of watchfulness,[15] are not only subject to be tempted, and quick to expose ourselves to temptations,[16] but also of ourselves unable and unwilling to resist them, to recover from them, and to use them

1 Matthew 6:12.
2 Psalm 130:3-4; Matthew 18:24-25; Romans 3:9-12,19.
3 Romans 3:24-26; Hebrews 9:22.
4 Ephesians 1:6-7.
5 2 Peter 1:2.
6 Jeremiah 14:7; Hosea 14:2.
7 Psalm 51:7-10,12; Romans 15:13.
8 Matthew 11:14-15; 18:35; Luke 11:4.
9 Matthew 6:13.
10 2 Chronicles 32:31.
11 1 Chronicles 21:1.
12 Mark 4:19; Luke 21:34.
13 James 1:14.
14 Galatians 5:17.
15 Matthew 26:41.
16 2 Chronicles 18:3; 19:2; Matthew 26:69-72; Galatians 2:11-14.

to our benefit;[1] and worthy to be left under the power of them;[2] we pray: that God would so overrule the world and all in it,[3] subdue the flesh,[4] and restrain Satan,[5] order all things,[6] bestow and bless all means of grace,[7] and alert us to watchfulness in the use of them, that we and all His people may by His providence be kept from being tempted to sin;[8] or, if tempted, that by His Spirit we may be powerfully supported and enabled to stand in the hour of temptation;[9] or, when fallen, raised again and recovered from it,[10] and have a sanctified use and benefit from it;[11] that our sanctification and salvation may be perfected,[12] Satan crushed under our feet,[13] and we fully freed from sin, temptation, and all evil forever.[14]

Q. 196. What does the conclusion of the Lord's Prayer teach us?

A. The conclusion of the Lord's Prayer (which is, "For yours is the kingdom and the power and the glory, forever. Amen."[15]), teaches us to enforce our petitions with arguments[16] that are to be taken, not from any worthiness in ourselves, or in any other creature, but from God,[17] and with our prayers to join praises,[18] ascribing to God alone eternal sovereignty, omnipotence, and glorious excellence;[19] in regard to which, as He is able and willing to help us,[20] so we by faith are emboldened to plead with Him that He would,[21] and to rely quietly on Him that he will, fulfill our requests.[22] And to testify our desires and assurance, we say, "Amen."[23]

1   1 Chronicles 21:1-4; 2 Chronicles 16:7-10; Romans 7:23-24.
2   Psalm 81:11-12.
3   John 17:15.
4   Psalm 51:10; 119:133.
5   2 Corinthians 12:7-8.
6   1 Corinthians 10:12-13.
7   Hebrews 13:20-21.
8   Psalm 19:13; Matthew 26:41.
9   Ephesians 3:14-17; 1 Thessalonians 3:13; Jude 24.
10   Psalm 51:12.
11   1 Peter 5:8-10.
12   2 Corinthians 13:7,9.
13   Zechariah 3:2; Luke 22:31-32; Romans 16:20.
14   John 17:15; 1 Thessalonians 5:23.
15   Matthew 6:13.
16   Romans 15:30.
17   Daniel 9:4,7-9,16-19.
18   Philippians 4:6.
19   1 Chronicles 29:10-13.
20   Luke 11:13; Ephesians 3:20-21.
21   2 Chronicles 20:6,11.
22   2 Chronicles 14:11.
23   1 Corinthians 14:16; Revelation 22:20-21.

The Westminster Shorter Catechism

The Rose Window and North Transept of Westminster where
William Wilberforce is buried next to his friend William Pitt the Younger.

Q. 1.   What is the chief end of man?

A.   Man's chief end is to glorify God,[1] and to enjoy him forever.[2]

Q. 2.   What rule has God given to direct us how we may glorify and enjoy him?

A.   The Word of God which is contained in the Scriptures of the Old and New Testaments[3] is the only rule to direct us how we may glorify and enjoy him.[4]

Q. 3.   What do the Scriptures principally teach?

A.   The Scriptures principally teach what man is to believe concerning God, and what duty God requires of man.[5]

Q. 4.   What is God?

A.   God is a Spirit,[6] infinite,[7] eternal[8] and unchangeable,[9] in his being,[10] wisdom,[11] power,[12] holiness,[13] justice, goodness, and truth.[14]

Q. 5.   Are there more Gods than one?

A.   There is but one only, the living and true God.[15]

Q. 6.   How many Persons are there in the Godhead?

A.   There are three Persons in the Godhead: the Father, the Son, and the Holy Spirit; and these three are one God, the same in substance, equal in power and glory.[16]

Q. 7.   What are the decrees of God?

A.   The decrees of God are His eternal purpose, according to the counsel of His will, by which, for His own glory, He has foreordained whatever comes to pass.[17]

Q. 8.   How does God execute His decrees?

A.   God executes His decrees in the works of creation and providence.

1   1 Corinthians 10:31.
2   Psalm 73:25-28.
3   Ephesians 2:20; 2 Timothy 3:16.
4   1 John 1:3-4.
5   2 Timothy 1:3; 3:16.
6   John 4:24.
7   Job 11:7-9.
8   Psalm 90:2.
9   James 1:17.
10   Exodus 3:14.
11   Psalm 117:5.
12   Revelation 4:8.
13   Revelation 15:4.
14   Exodus 34:6-7.
15   Deuteronomy 6:4.
16   Matthew 28:19; 1 John 5:7.
17   Romans 9:22-23; Ephesians 1:4,11.

Q. 9.   What is the work of creation?

A.   The work of creation is God's making all things from nothing, by the word of His power, in the space of six days, and all very good.[1]

Q. 10.   How did God create man?

A.   God created man male and female, after His own image, in knowledge, righteousness, and holiness, with dominion over the creatures.[2]

Q. 11.   What are God's works of providence?

A.   God's works of providence are His most holy,[3] wise,[4] and powerful preserving[5] and governing all His creatures, and all their actions.[6]

Q. 12.   What special act of providence did God exercise toward man, in the estate in which he was created?

A.   When God created man, He entered into a covenant of life with him, on condition of perfect obedience; forbidding him to eat of the Tree of the Knowledge of Good and Evil, on the pain of death.[7]

Q. 13.   Did our first parents continue in the estate in which they were created?

A.   Our first parents, being left to the freedom of their own will, fell from the estate in which they were created, by sinning against God.[8]

Q. 14.   What is sin?

A.   Sin is any lack of conformity to, or transgression of, the law of God.[9]

Q. 15.   What was the sin by which our first parents fell from the estate in which they were created?

A.   The sin by which our first parents fell from the estate in which they were created was their eating of the forbidden fruit.[10]

---

1   Genesis 1; Hebrews 11:3.
2   Genesis 1:26-28; Ephesians 4:24; Colossians 3:10.
3   Psalm 145:17.
4   Psalm 104:24; Isaiah 28:29.
5   Hebrews 1:3.
6   Psalm 103:19; Matthew 10:29-31.
7   Genesis 2:17; Galatians 3:12.
8   Genesis 3:6-8,13; Ecclesiastes 7:29.
9   1 John 3:4.
10   Genesis 3:6.

Q. 16. Did all mankind fall in Adam's first transgression?

A. The covenant being made with Adam, not only for himself, but for his descendants, all mankind, descending from him by ordinary generation, sinned in him, and fell with him, in his first transgression.[1]

Q. 17. Into what estate did the Fall bring mankind?

A. The Fall brought mankind into an estate of sin and misery.[2]

Q. 18. What is the sinfulness of that estate into which man fell?

A. The sinfulness of that estate into which man fell consists of: the guilt of Adam's first sin, the lack of original righteousness, and the corruption of his whole nature, which is commonly called original sin, together with all actual transgressions that proceed from it.[3]

Q. 19. What is the misery of that estate into which man fell?

A. All mankind, by their fall, lost communion with God,[4] are under His wrath and curse,[5] and so made liable to all miseries of this life, to death itself, and to the pains of hell forever.[6]

Q. 20. Did God leave all mankind to perish in the estate of sin and misery?

A. God, having out of his mere good pleasure, from all eternity, elected some to everlasting life,[7] did enter into a covenant of grace, to deliver them out of the estate of sin and misery, and to bring them into an estate of salvation by a Redeemer.[8]

Q. 21. Who is the Redeemer of God's elect?

A. The only Redeemer of God's elect is the Lord Jesus Christ,[9] who, being the eternal Son of God, became man,[10] and so was, and continues to be, God and man, in two distinct natures, and one Person forever.[11]

---

1 Genesis 2:16-17; Romans 5:12; 1 Corinthians 15:21-22.

2 Romans 5:12.

3 Matthew 15:19; Romans 5:10-20; 5:12,19; Ephesians 2:1-3; James 1:14-15.

4 Genesis 3:8,10,24.

5 Galatians 3:10; Ephesians 2:2-3.

6 Lamentations 3:39; Matthew 25:41,46; Romans 6:23.

7 Ephesians 1:4.

8 Romans 3:20-22; Galatians 3:21-22.

9 1 Timothy 2:5-6.

10 John 1:14; Galatians 4:4.

11 Luke 1:35; Romans 9:5; Colossians 2:9; Hebrews 7:24-25.

Q. 22.   How did Christ, being the Son of God, become man?

A.   Christ, the Son of God, became man, by taking to Himself a true body[1] and a reasonable soul,[2] being conceived by the power of the Holy Spirit, in the womb of the Virgin Mary, and born of her,[3] yet without sin.[4]

Q. 23.   What offices does Christ execute as our Redeemer?

A.   Christ, as our Redeemer, executes the offices of a prophet, of a priest, and of a king, both in His estate of humiliation and exaltation.[5]

Q. 24.   How does Christ execute the office of a prophet?

A.   Christ executes the office of a prophet in revealing to us, by His Word and Spirit, the will of God for our salvation.[6]

Q. 25.   How does Christ execute the office of a priest?

A.   Christ executes the office of a priest in his once offering up of Himself a sacrifice to satisfy divine justice,[7] and reconcile us to God,[8] and in making continual intercession for us.[9]

Q. 26.   How does Christ execute the office of a king?

A.   Christ executes the office of a king in subduing us to Himself,[10] in ruling[11] and defending us,[12] and in restraining and conquering all His and our enemies.[13]

Q. 27.   What was Christ's humiliation?

A.   Christ's humiliation consisted in His being born, and that in a low condition,[14] made under the law,[15] undergoing the miseries of this life,[16] the wrath of God,[17] and the cursed death of the cross;[18] in being buried,[19] and continuing under the power of death for a time.[20]

---

1   Hebrews 2:14,16; 10:5.
2   Matthew 26:38.
3   Luke 1:27,31,35,42; Galatians 4:4.
4   Hebrews 4:15; 7:26.
5   Psalm 2:6,8-11; Isaiah 9:6-7; Matthew 21:5; Acts 3:21-22; 2 Corinthians 13:3; Hebrews 5:5-7; 7:25; 12:25.
6   John 1:18; 15:15; 20:31; 1 Peter 1:10-12.
7   Hebrews 9:14,28.
8   Hebrews 2:17.
9   Hebrews 7:24-25.
10 Acts 15:14-16.
11 Isaiah 32:22.
12 Isaiah 32:1-2.
13 Psalm 110; 1 Corinthians 15:25.
14 Luke 2:7.
15 Galatians 4:4.
16 Isaiah 53:2-3; Hebrews 12:2-3.
17 Matthew 27:46; Luke 22:44.
18 Philippians 2:8.
19 1 Corinthians 15:3-4.
20 Acts 2:24-27,31.

Q. 28.   What is Christ's exaltation?

A.   Christ's exaltation consists in His rising again from the dead on the third day,[1] in ascending into heaven,[2] in sitting at the right hand of God the Father,[3] and in coming to judge the world at the last day.[4]

Q. 29.   How do we take part in the redemption purchased by Christ?

A.   We take part in the redemption purchased by Christ by the effectual application of it to us[5] by His Holy Spirit.[6]

Q. 30.   How does the Spirit apply to us the redemption purchased by Christ?

A.   The Spirit applies to us the redemption purchased by Christ by working faith in us,[7] and thereby uniting us to Christ in our effectual calling.[8]

Q. 31.   What is effectual calling?

A.   Effectual calling is the work of God's Spirit,[9] by which, convincing us of our sin and misery,[10] enlightening our minds in the knowledge of Christ,[11] and renewing our wills,[12] he persuades and enables us to embrace Jesus Christ, freely offered to us in the Gospel.[13]

Q. 32.   What benefits are there in this life for those who are effectually called?

A.   Those who are effectually called partake in justification,[14] adoption,[15] sanctification, and the other benefits that, in this life, do either accompany them or flow from them.[16]

Q. 33.   What is justification?

A.   Justification is an act of God's free grace, in which He pardons all our sins,[17] and accepts us as righteous in His sight,[18] only

1   1 Corinthians 15:4.
2   Mark 16:19.
3   Ephesians 1:20.
4   Acts 1:11; 17:31.
5   John 1:11-12.
6   Titus 3:5-6.
7   John 6:37-39; Ephesians 1:13-14; 2:8.
8   1 Corinthians 1:9; Ephesians 3:17.
9   2 Thessalonians 2:13-14; 2 Timothy 1:9.
10 Acts 2:37.
11 Acts 26:18.
12 Ezekiel 36:26-27.
13 John 6:44-45; Philippians 2:13.
14 Romans 8:30.
15 Ephesians 1:5.
16 1 Corinthians 1:26,30.
17 Romans 3:24-25; 4:6-8.
18 2 Corinthians 5:19,21.

for the righteousness of Christ imputed to us,[1] and received by faith alone.[2]

Q. 34. What is adoption?

A. Adoption is an act of God's free grace,[3] by which we are received as sons of God, and have a right to all the privileges of that standing.[4]

Q. 35. What is sanctification?

A. Sanctification is the work of God's free grace,[5] by which we are renewed in the whole man after the image of God,[6] and are enabled more and more to die to sin and live to righteousness.[7]

Q. 36. What are the benefits that in this life accompany or flow from justification, adoption, and sanctification?

A. The benefits that in this life do accompany or flow from justification, adoption, and sanctification are: assurance of God's love, peace of conscience,[8] joy in the Holy Spirit,[9] increase of grace,[10] and perseverance to the end.[11]

Q. 37. What benefits do believers receive from Christ at death?

A. The souls of believers are at their deaths made perfect in holiness,[12] and do immediately pass into glory;[13] and their bodies, being still united to Christ,[14] do rest in their graves[15] till the resurrection.[16]

Q. 38. What benefits do believers receive from Christ at the resurrection?

A. At the resurrection, believers, being raised up in glory,[17] shall be openly acknowledged and acquitted in the day of judgment,[18] and made perfectly blessed in the full enjoying of God[19] to all eternity.[20]

1   Romans 5:17-19.
2   Galatians 2:16; Philippians 3:9.
3   1 John 3:1.
4   John 1:12; Romans 8:17.
5   2 Thessalonians 2:13.
6   Ephesians 4:23-24.
7   Romans 6:4,6; 8:1.
8   Romans 5:1-2,5.
9   Romans 14:17.
10 Proverbs 4:18.
11 1 Peter 1:5; 1 John 5:13.
12 Hebrews 12:23.
13 Luke 23:43; 2 Corinthians 5:1,6,8; Philippians 1:23.
14 1 Thessalonians 4:14.
15 Isaiah 57:2.
16 Job 19:26-27.
17 1 Corinthians 15:43.
18 Matthew 10:32; 25:23.
19 1 Corinthians 13:12; 1 John 3:2.
20 1 Thessalonians 4:17-18.

Q. 39.   What is the duty that God requires of man?
A.   The duty that God requires of man is obedience to His revealed
         will.[1]

Q. 40.   What did God at first reveal to man for the rule of his obedi-
         ence?
A.   The rule that God at first revealed to man for his obedience was
         the moral law.[2]

Q. 41.   Where is the moral law found to be summarized?
A.   The moral law is found summarized in the Ten Command-
         ments.[3]

Q. 42.   What is the sum of the Ten Commandments?
A.   The sum of the Ten Commandments is: to love the Lord our
         God with all our heart, with all our soul, with all our strength,
         and with all our mind; and our neighbor as ourselves.[4]

Q. 43.   What is the preface to the Ten Commandments?
A.   The preface to the Ten Commandments is in these words: "I am
         the LORD your God, who brought you out of the land of Egypt,
         out of the house of slavery."[5]

Q. 44.   What does the preface to the Ten Commandments
         teach us?
A.   The preface to the Ten Commandments teaches us that because
         God is the Lord, and our God and Redeemer, therefore we are
         bound to keep all His commandments.[6]

Q. 45.   Which is the First Commandment?
A.   The First Commandment is, "You shall have no other gods
         before me."[7]

1   1 Samuel 15:22; Micah 6:8.
2   Romans 2:14-15; 10:5.
3   Deuteronomy 10:4; Matthew 19:17.
4   Matthew 2:37-40.
5   Exodus 20:2 (English Standard Version).
6   Luke 1:74-75; 1 Peter 1:15-18.
7   Exodus 20:3.

Q. 46.   What is required in the First Commandment?

A.   The First Commandment requires us to know and acknowledge
         God to be the only true God, and our God;[1] and to worship
         and glorify Him accordingly.[2]

Q. 47.   What is forbidden in the First Commandment?

A.   The First Commandment forbids the denying,[3] or not worship-
         ing and glorifying, the true God as God,[4] and our God;[5] and
         the giving to any other of that worship and glory due to Him
         alone.[6]

Q. 48.   What are we especially taught by the words, "before me," in
         the First Commandment?

A.   These words, "before me," in the First Commandment teach us
         that God, who sees all things, takes notice of, and is much dis-
         pleased with, the sin of having any other god.[7]

Q. 49.   Which is the Second Commandment?

A.   The Second Commandment is, "You shall not make for yourself
         a carved image, or any likeness of anything that is in heaven
         above, or that is in the earth beneath, or that is in the water
         under the earth. You shall not bow down to them or serve
         them, for I the LORD your God am a jealous God, visiting the
         iniquity of the fathers on the children to the third and the fourth
         generation of those who hate me, but showing steadfast love to
         thousands of those who love me and keep my command-
         ments."[8]

Q. 50.   What is required in the Second Commandment?

A.   The Second Commandment requires the receiving, observing,
         and keeping pure and entire all such religious worship and
         ordinances as God has appointed in His Word.[9]

---

1   Deuteronomy 26:17; 1 Chronicles 28:9.
2   Psalm 29:2; Matthew 4:10.
3   Psalm 14:1.
4   Roman 1:21.
5   Psalm 81:10-11.
6   Romans 1:25-26.
7   Psalm 46:20-21; Ezekiel 8:5-6.
8   Exodus 20:4-6 (ESV).
9   Deuteronomy 32:46; Matthew 28:20; Acts 2:42.

Q. 51.   What is forbidden in the Second Commandment?

A.   The Second Commandment forbids the worshiping of God by images,[1] or any other way not appointed in His Word.[2]

Q. 52.   What are the reasons attached to the Second Commandment?

A.   The reasons attached to the Second Commandment are: God's sovereignty over us,[3] His ownership in us,[4] and the zeal he has for His own worship.[5]

Q. 53.   Which is the Third Commandment?

A.   The Third Commandment is, "You shall not take the name of the LORD your God in vain, for the LORD will not hold him guiltless who takes his name in vain."[6]

Q. 54.   What is required in the Third Commandment?

A.   The Third Commandment requires the holy and reverent use of God's names,[7] titles,[8] attributes,[9] ordinances,[10] Word,[11] and works.[12]

Q. 55.   What is forbidden in the Third Commandment?

A.   The Third Commandment forbids all profaning or abusing of anything by which God makes Himself known.[13]

Q. 56.   What is the reason attached to the Third Commandment?

A.   The reason attached to the Third Commandment is that, however those who break this commandment may escape punishment from men, yet the Lord our God will not allow them to escape His righteous judgment.[14]

Q. 57.   Which is the Fourth Commandment?

A.   The Fourth Commandment is, "Remember the Sabbath day, to keep it holy. Six days you shall labor, and do all your work, but the seventh day is a Sabbath to the LORD your God. On it you

---

1   Exodus 32:5,8; Deuteronomy 4:15-19.
2   Deuteronomy 11:31-32.
3   Psalm 95:2-3.
4   Psalm 45:11.
5   Exodus 34:13-14.
6   Exodus 20:7 (ESV).
7   Deuteronomy 28:58; Matthew 6:9.
8   Psalm 68:4.
9   Revelation 15:3-4.
10   Malachi 1:11,14.
11   Psalm 138:1-2.
12   Job 26:24.
13   Malachi 1:6-7,12; 2:2; 3:14.
14   Deuteronomy 28:58-59;
     1 Samuel 2:12,17,22,29; 3:13.

shall not do any work, you, or your son, or your daughter, your
male servant, or your female servant, or your livestock, or the
sojourner who is within your gates. For in six days the LORD
made heaven and earth, the sea, and all that is in them, and
rested the seventh day. Therefore the LORD blessed the Sabbath day and made it holy."[1]

Q. 58. What is required in the Fourth Commandment?

A.   The Fourth Commandment requires the keeping holy to God
        such set times as He has appointed in His Word; expressly one
        whole day in seven, to be a holy Sabbath to Himself.[2]

Q. 59. Which day of the seven has God appointed to be the weekly
        Sabbath?

A.   From the beginning of the world to the resurrection of Christ,
        God appointed the seventh day of the week to be the weekly
        Sabbath; and the first day of the week ever since, to continue to
        the end of the world, which is the Christian Sabbath.[3]

Q. 60. How is the Sabbath to be sanctified?

A.   The Sabbath is to be sanctified by a holy resting all that day,[4]
        even from such worldly employments and recreations as are
        lawful on other days;[5] and spending the whole time in the
        public and private exercises of God's worship,[6] except so much
        as is to be taken up in the works of necessity and mercy.[7]

Q. 61. What is forbidden in the Fourth Commandment?

A.   The Fourth Commandment forbids the omission, or careless
        performance, of the duties required,[8] and the profaning the
        day by idleness,[9] or doing that which is in itself sinful,[10] or

---

1   Exodus 20:8-11(ESV).
2   Deuteronomy 5:12-14.
3   Genesis 2:2-3; Acts 20:7; 1 Corinthians 16:1-2.
4   Exodus 16:25-28; 20:8,10.
5   Nehemiah 13:15-19.
6   Psalm 92; Isaiah 66:23; Luke 4:16; Acts 20:7.
7   Matthew 12:1-31.
8   Ezekiel 22:26; Amos 8:5; Malachi 1:13.
9   Acts 20:7,9.
10 Ezekiel 23:38.

by unnecessary thoughts, words, or works, about our worldly employments or recreations.[1]

Q. 62. What are the reasons attached to the Fourth Commandment?
A. The reasons attached to the Fourth Commandment are: God's allowing us six days of the week for our own employments,[2] His establishment of a special ownership in the seventh, His own example, and His blessing the Sabbath day.[3]

Q. 63. Which is the Fifth Commandment?
A. The Fifth Commandment is, "Honor your father and your mother, that your days may be long in the land that the LORD your God is giving you."[4]

Q. 64. What is required in the Fifth Commandment?
A. The Fifth Commandment requires the preserving of the honor, and performing the duties, belonging to everyone in their various situations and relationships, as superiors,[5] inferiors,[6] or equals.[7]

Q. 65. What is forbidden in the Fifth Commandment?
A. The Fifth Commandment forbids the neglecting of, or doing anything against, the honor and duty that belong to everyone in their various situations and relationships.[8]

Q. 66. What is the reason attached to the Fifth Commandment?
A. The reason attached to the Fifth Commandment is a promise of long life and prosperity (as far as it shall serve for God's glory, and their own good) to all who keep this commandment.[9]

Q. 67. Which is the Sixth Commandment?
A. The Sixth Commandment is, "You shall not murder."[10]

1 Isaiah 58:13; Jeremiah 17:24-26.
2 Exodus 20:9.
3 Exodus 20:11.
4 Exodus 20:12 (ESV).
5 Ephesians 5:21.
6 1 Peter 2:17.
7 Romans 12:10.
8 Ezekiel 34:2-4; Matthew 15:4-6; Romans 13:8.
9 Deuteronomy 5:16; Ephesians 6:2-3.
10 Exodus 20:13 (ESV).

Q. 68. What is required in the Sixth Commandment?

A. The Sixth Commandment requires all lawful endeavors to preserve our own lives,[1] and the lives of others.[2]

Q. 69. What is forbidden in the Sixth Commandment?

A. The Sixth Commandment forbids the taking away of our own lives or the lives of our neighbors unjustly, or whatever tends to do so.[3]

Q. 70. Which is the Seventh Commandment?

A. The Seventh Commandment is, "You shall not commit adultery."[4]

Q. 71. What is required in the Seventh Commandment?

A. The Seventh Commandment requires the preservation of our own and our neighbor's chastity, in heart, speech, and behavior.[5]

Q. 72. What is forbidden in the Seventh Commandment?

A. The Seventh Commandment forbids all unchaste thoughts, words, and actions.[6]

Q. 73. Which is the Eighth Commandment?

A. The Eighth Commandment is, "You shall not steal."[7]

Q. 74. What is required in the Eighth Commandment?

A. The Eighth Commandment requires that we utilize only lawful means in obtaining and furthering the wealth and outward estate of ourselves and others.[8]

Q. 75. What is forbidden in the Eighth Commandment?

A. The Eighth Commandment forbids whatever does, or may, unjustly hinder our own, or our neighbor's, wealth or outward estate.[9]

1 Ephesians 5:28-29.
2 1 Kings 13:4.
3 Genesis 9:6; Acts 16:28.
4 Exodus 20:14 (ESV).
5 1 Corinthians 7:2-3,5,34,36; Colossians 4:6; 1 Peter 3:2.
6 Matthew 5:28; Matthew 15:19.
7 Exodus 20:15 (ESV).
8 Genesis 30:30; 47:14,20; Exodus 23:4-5; Leviticus 25:35; Deuteronomy 22:1-5; 1 Timothy 5:8.
9 Proverbs 21:17; 23:20-21; 28:19; Ephesians 4:28.

Q. 76.   Which is the Ninth Commandment?

A.   The Ninth Commandment is, "You shall not bear false witness against your neighbor."[1]

Q. 77.   What is required in the Ninth Commandment?

A.   The Ninth Commandment requires the maintaining and promoting of truth between man and man,[2] and of our own and our neighbor's good name,[3] especially in testifying as witnesses.[4]

Q. 78.   What is forbidden in the Ninth Commandment?

A.   The Ninth Commandment forbids whatever is prejudicial to truth, or injurious to our own or our neighbor's good name.[5]

Q. 79.   Which is the Tenth Commandment?

A.   The Tenth Commandment is, "You shall not covet your neighbor's house; you shall not covet your neighbor's wife, or his male servant, or his female servant, or his ox, or his donkey, or anything that is your neighbor's."[6]

Q. 80.   What is required in the Tenth Commandment?

A.   The Tenth Commandment requires full contentment with our own condition,[7] with a right and charitable frame of spirit toward our neighbor and all that is his.[8]

Q. 81.   What is forbidden in the Tenth Commandment?

A.   The Tenth Commandment forbids all discontentment with our own estate,[9] envying or grieving at the good of our neighbor,[10] and all unreasonable motions and affections toward anything that is his.[11]

---

1   Exodus 20:16 (ESV).
2   Zechariah 8:16.
3   3 John 12.
4   Proverbs 14:5,25.
5   Leviticus 19:16; 1 Samuel 17:28; Psalm 15:3.
6   Exodus 20:17 (ESV).

7   1 Timothy 6:6; Hebrews 13:5.
8   Job 31:29; Romans 12:15; 1 Corinthians 13:4-7; 1 Timothy 50:5.
9   1 Kings 21:4; Esther 5:13; 1 Corinthians 10:10.
10   Galatians 5:26; James 3:14,16.
11   Deuteronomy 5:21; Romans 7:7-8; 13:9.

Q. 82. Is any man able to keep perfectly the commandments of God?

A. No mere man, since the Fall, is able, in this life, to keep perfectly the commandments of God,[1] but does break them daily, in thought, word, and deed.[2]

Q. 83. Are all transgressions of the law equally wicked?

A. Some sins in themselves, and by reason of aggravating circumstances, are more wicked in the sight of God than others.[3]

Q. 84. What does every sin deserve?

A. Every sin deserves God's wrath and curse, both in this life and that which is to come.[4]

Q. 85. What does God require of us, that we may escape his wrath and curse, due to us for sin?

A. To escape the wrath and curse of God, due to us for sin, God requires of us faith in Jesus Christ, repentance to life,[5] with the diligent use of all the outward means by which Christ communicates to us the benefits of redemption.[6]

Q. 86. What is faith in Jesus Christ?

A. Faith in Jesus Christ is a saving grace,[7] by which we receive and rest on Him alone for salvation, as He is offered to us in the Gospel.[8]

Q. 87. What is repentance to life?

A. Repentance to life is a saving grace,[9] by which a sinner, out of a true sense of his sin,[10] and understanding of the mercy of God in Christ,[11] does, with grief and hatred of his sin, turn from it to God,[12] with full intention of, and endeavor after, new obedience.[13]

---

1   Ecclesiastes 7:20; Galatians 5:17; 1 John 1:8,10.
2   Genesis 6:5; 8:21; Romans 3:9-21; James 3:2-13.
3   Psalm 78:17,32,56; Ezekiel 8:6,13,15;
    1 John 5:16.
4   Lamentations 3:39; Matthew 25:41;
    Galatians 3:10; Ephesians 5:6.
5   Acts 20:21.
6   Proverbs 2:1-5; 8:33-36; Isaiah 55:3.

78 Isaiah 26:3-4; John 1:12; Galatians 2:16;
    Philippians 3:9.
9   Acts 11:18.
10 Acts 2:37-38.
11 Jeremiah 3:22; Joel 2:12.
12 Jeremiah 31:18-19; Ezekiel 36:31.
13 Isaiah 1:16-17; 2 Corinthians 7:11.

Q. 88.   What are the outward means by which Christ communicates to us the benefits of redemption?

A.   The outward and ordinary means by which Christ communicates to us the benefits of redemption are His ordinances, especially the Word, sacraments, and prayer, all of which are made effectual to the elect for salvation.[1]

Q. 89.   How is the Word made effectual to salvation?

A.   The Spirit of God makes the reading, but especially the preaching, of the Word an effectual means of convincing and converting sinners, and of building them up in holiness and comfort, through faith to salvation.[2]

Q. 90.   How is the Word to be read and heard, that it may become effectual to salvation?

A.   That the Word may become effectual to salvation we must attend to it with diligence,[3] preparation,[4] and prayer;[5] receive it with faith and love;[6] lay it up in our hearts;[7] and practice it in our lives.[8]

Q. 91.   How do the sacraments become effectual means of salvation?

A.   The sacraments become effectual means of salvation, not from any virtue in them, or in him who administers them, but only by the blessing of Christ,[9] and the working of His Spirit in those who by faith receive them.[10]

Q. 92.   What is a sacrament?

A.   A sacrament is a holy ordinance instituted by Christ, in which, by perceptible signs, Christ and the benefits of the new covenant are represented, sealed, and applied to believers.[11]

---

1   Matthew 28:19-20; Acts 2:42,46-47.
2   Nehemiah 8:8; Psalms 19:8; Acts 20:32; 26:18; Romans 1:16; 10:13-17; 15:4; 1 Corinthians 14:24-25; 2 Timothy 3:15-17.
3   Proverbs 8:34.
4   1 Peter 2:1-2.
5   Psalm 119:18.
6   2 Thessalonians 2:10; Hebrews 4:2.
7   Psalm 119:11.
8   Luke 8:15; James 1:25.
9   Matthew 3:11; 1 Corinthians 3:6-7; 1 Peter 3:21.
10   1 Corinthians 12:13.
11   Genesis 17:7,10; Exodus 12; 1 Corinthians 11:23,26.

Q. 93. Which are the sacraments of the New Testament?

A. The sacraments of the New Testament are Baptism[1] and the Lord's Supper.[2]

Q. 94. What is Baptism?

A. Baptism is a sacrament, in which the washing with water, in the name of the Father, and of the Son, and of the Holy Spirit,[3] does signify and seal our grafting into Christ, and receiving of the benefits of the Covenant of Grace, and our engagement to be the Lord's.[4]

Q. 95. To whom is Baptism to be administered?

A. Baptism is not to be administered to any who are out of the visible church, till they profess their faith in Christ and obedience to him;[5] but the infants of those who are members of the visible Church are to be baptized.[6]

Q. 96. What is the Lord's Supper?

A. The Lord's Supper is a sacrament, in which by giving and receiving bread and wine, according to Christ's direction, His death is shown forth; and the worthy receivers are, not after a corporal and carnal manner, but by faith, made partakers of His body and blood, with all His benefits, to their spiritual nourishment and growth in grace.[7]

Q. 97. What is required to be worthy of receiving the Lord's Supper?

A. It is required of those who would receive the Lord's Supper worthily that they examine themselves, as to their knowledge to discern the Lord's body,[8] as to their faith to feed on Him,[9] and as to their repentance,[10] love,[11] and new obedience;[12] lest, coming unworthily, they eat and drink judgment on themselves.[13]

---

1 Matthew 28:19.
2 Matthew 26:26-28.
3 Matthew 28:19.
4 Romans 6:4; Galatians 3:27.
5 Acts 2:38; 8:36-38.
6 Genesis 17:10; Acts 2:38-39;
   1 Corinthians 7:14; Colossians 2:11-12.
7 1 Corinthians 11:23-26.
8 1 Corinthians 11:28-29.
9 2 Corinthians 13:5.
10 1 Corinthians 11:31.
11 1 Corinthians 10:16-17.
12 1 Corinthians 5:7-8.
13 1 Corinthians 11:28-29.

Q. 98. What is prayer?

A. Prayer is an offering up of our desires to God,[1] for things agreeable to His will,[2] in the name of Christ,[3] with confession of our
sins,[4] and thankful acknowledgment of His mercies.[5]

Q. 99. What rule has God given for our direction in prayer?

A. The whole Word of God is of use to direct us in prayer;[6] but
the special rule of direction is the form of prayer that Christ
taught His disciples, commonly called "the Lord's Prayer."[7]

Q. 100. What does the preface of the Lord's Prayer teach us?

A. The preface of the Lord's Prayer, which is, "Our Father in
heaven,"[8] teaches us to draw near to God with all holy reverence and confidence, as children to a father, able and ready to
help us;[9] and that we should pray with and for others.[10]

Q. 101. For what do we pray in the first petition?

A. In the first petition, which is, "Hallowed be your name,"[11] we
pray that God would enable us, and others, to glorify Him in all
the means by which he makes Himself known,[12] and that he
would arrange all things to His own glory.[13]

Q. 102. For what do we pray in the second petition?

A. In the second petition, which is, "Your kingdom come,"[14] we
pray that Satan's kingdom may be destroyed,[15] and that the
kingdom of grace may be advanced,[16] ourselves and others
brought into it, and kept in it,[17] and that the kingdom of glory
may be hastened.[18]

Q. 103. For what do we pray in the third petition?

A. In the third petition, which is, "Your will be done, on earth as it
is in heaven, "[19] we pray that God, by His grace, would make

1   Psalm 62:8.
2   1 John 5:14.
3   John 16:23.
4   Psalm 32:5-6; Daniel 9:4.
5   Philippians 4:6.
6   1 John 5:14.
7   Matthew 6:9-13; Luke 11:2-4.
8   Matthew 6:9.
9   Luke 11:13; Romans 8:15.
10 Acts 12:5; 1 Timothy 2:1-2.
11 Matthew 6:9.
12 Psalm 67:2-3.
13 Psalm 83.
14 Matthew 6:10.
15 Psalm 68:1,18.
16 Revelation 12:10-11.
17 John 17:9,20; Romans 10:1;
    2 Thessalonians 3:1.
18 Revelation 22:20.
19 Matthew 6:10.

us able and willing to know, obey, and submit to His will in all things,[1] as the angels do in heaven.[2]

Q. 104. For what do we pray in the fourth petition?

A. In the fourth petition, which is, "Give us this day our daily bread,"[3] we pray that, of God's free gift, we may receive a sufficient portion of the good things of this life, and enjoy His blessing with them.[4]

Q. 105. For what do we pray in the fifth petition?

A. In the fifth petition, which is, "Forgive us our debts, as we also have forgiven our debtors,"[5] we pray that God, for Christ's sake, would freely pardon all our sins;[6] which we are more encouraged to ask because by His grace we are enabled from the heart to forgive others.[7]

Q. 106. For what do we pray in the sixth petition?

A. In the sixth petition, which is, "And lead us not into temptation, but deliver us from evil,"[8] we pray that God would either keep us from being tempted to sin,[9] or support and deliver us when we are tempted.[10]

Q. 107. What does the conclusion of the Lord's Prayer teach us?

A. The conclusion of the Lord's Prayer, which is, "For yours is the kingdom and the power and the glory, forever. Amen,"[11] teaches us to take our encouragement in prayer from God only,[12] and in our prayers to praise Him, ascribing kingdom, power, and glory to Him;[13] and in testimony of our desire and assurance to be heard, we say, "Amen."[14]

1	2 Samuel 15:25; Job 1:21; Psalm 67; 119:36; Matthew 26:39.	7	Matthew 13:35; Luke 11:4.
2	Psalm 103:20-21.	8	Matthew 6:13.
3	Matthew 6:11.	9	Matthew 26:41.
4	Genesis 28:23; Proverbs 30:8-9; 1 Timothy 4:4-5.	10	2 Corinthians 12:7-8.
5	Matthew 6:12.	11	Matthew 6:13.
6	Psalm 51:1-2,7,9; Daniel 9:17-19.	13	Daniel 9:4,7-9,16-19.
		13	1 Chronicles 29:10-13.
		14	1 Corinthians 14:16; Revelation 22:20-21.